Haunted Henry County

And Nearby Hoosier Haunts. Mysteries, Legends and Personal Accounts of the Paranormal

by

Charlene Z. Perry

authorHOUSE™

1663 LIBERTY DRIVE, SUITE 200
BLOOMINGTON, INDIANA 47403
(800) 839-8640
WWW.AUTHORHOUSE.COM

First published by AuthorHouse 09/29/04

ISBN: 1-4184-8574-8 (sc)

Library of Congress Control Number: 2004095688

Printed in the United States of America
Bloomington, Indiana

This book is printed on acid-free paper.

Front Cover: This peaceful Henry County lane, enveloped in a golden mist, was the scene of a tragic murder many years ago. The photograph was the only one, in a roll of twenty-seven films, in which this eerie glow occurred.

Dedicated to:

The generous individuals who shared their stories with me.
and
To those who never got a chance to speak for themselves:
Catherine, Pearlie, Lova, Virginia and Alice Jean, and Molly
and her baby.
and
To Miss F-32, (Lady in the Mist), Our Little Friend, and the Little
Ghost Girl, whoever you are.

Acknowledgments

Many thanks for the help and information given to me by the following: Marjorie Wilkinson, Knightstown Public Library. The Book Mark, Knightstown. Marilyn Manning , Glen Cove Cemetery. Staff of South Mound Cemetery. Spiceland Public Library. Henry County Historical Society. Margret Swim. Tom Saunders. Donna Tauber. Rick Sweigart. Christy White. Darrell Deck. D.S. Bowen. Richmond Historical Society. Marilyn, Garon and Steve of Morrison Reeves Library, Richmond. Roberta Lemly, Phyllis Harrod, Sarah Addison and Patty Hershberger of the History Room, Cambridge City Public Library. Norma Jean Smith, local historian, Dublin. Kamala Narajanan, Dublin Public Library. Rush County Public Library. Fayette County Public Library. Wayne Goodman, Historic Landmarks Foundation. Pat, Deb and Mary Lou, Muncie Public Library Genealogy Center. Staff of Elm Ridge Cemetery, Muncie. Mary Beth, Mark, Heidi, Pat and Paul, and the members of the Board of Trustees of Camp Chesterfield. Jamey Hickson, Heritage Librarian at Boone County Public Library, Lebanon, Indiana. Joy Summers, Greenfield Public Library. Fairmount Public Library. Fairmount Historical Museum. Judy Cowling, Historic Fairmount. David Loehr, James Dean Gallery. Mark Kinniman, Nostalgia Unlimited. Sara and Randy Ballinger, Walnut Creek /Club Run Golf Course. Suzanne Robinson and Marilyn Engle, Lynn Public Library. Kimball Hendrix. Macinda and Linda at CVS… and my daughter, Lisa Perry Martin and her husband David Martin, for their help with the "Lady in the Mist." (Miss F32)

*****A special "thank you" to the staff of the New Castle Henry County Public Library for their constant help and support during the writing of this book.

Contents

Introduction

This is a collection of thirty-seven local and regional ghost stories, legends, and mysteries. The local ghost stories have been related as true accounts. I personally interviewed each participant and did research whenever research material was available. Often I took photographs and audio-taped the interview.

Henry County ghosts are similar to ghosts the world over. And like all other ghosts, many appear to have definite purposes. Some entities seem to be here to help, comfort or reassure, such as the woman in "Lady in Black." Some are frightening and repeat aimless gestures, such as the entities in "Haunted House at Flatrock." Others seem to have a specific one-time mission, as the "ghost" in "The Repentant Friend." There are those that seem lost or lonely, such as the little boy in "Our Little Friend.", or the child in "Little Ghost Girl."

Like all ghosts, Henry County ghosts are found in old houses, (and sometimes new houses) cemeteries, schools, orphanages, funeral homes, nursing homes, and in places where there has been tragedy and violence.

Many local people had ghost stories to tell. Those interviewed came from varied economic, social and religious backgrounds. They are people you may know. They could be a co-worker, an acquaintance or a neighbor. For persons who did not want their real names used, I placed an asterisk above a fictitious name. In certain stories, I omitted the owner's name and address when mentioning a specific house or area, if it would have invaded privacy.

The mysteries are factual and have been backed up by research and interviews when possible. The legends were also researched. An attempt was made to determine the source and truth of the legend. Not all of our Henry County legends are included, either because there was not enough available material or enough time.

I wrote this book because I find reading true ghost stories intriguing and entertaining. I also have a deep curiosity about the paranormal world, and especially what causes "ghosts" and "hauntings."

Many "haunted" houses have a history of tragedy. (murder, suicide, prolonged sickness, depression, or mental illness.) The tragic death of a child or young person or the presence of a disturbed adolescent seems to increase the chances of paranormal activities in a house.

My first personal encounter with the paranormal came some years ago when I moved into a New Castle house which was associated with the disappearance of a little girl. My experience is told in the story, "The House That Spoke." I knew the history of the house when I bought it, but being a strong person and not easily intimidated, I did not believe it would affect me. I learned, though, that daily contact in such an atmosphere can be emotionally and physically debilitating.

Fortunately, the field of the paranormal is now receiving serious study by many qualified researchers and investigators. There are ghost tracking groups and other organizations in existence today, which are making a serious effort to study the field objectively, and to teach other would-be researchers how to determine the real from the counterfeit. I believe that, in the near future, satisfactory explanations will be found for much of the unusual psychic phenomena that some of us we now find frightening or mystifying.

The most encouraging and comforting aspect of the paranormal is its suggestion of intriguing spiritual dimensions of which we may still be unaware. Most important, it offers the hope that the human spirit survives the transition of physical death.

This is a newspaper photograph of Catherine, Dr. and Mrs. Winters, and the Winters home in 1914, at the time of the arrest of the Winters. Credit: Illinois Historical Society.

The Mysterious Disappearance of Catherine Winters

Many local people believe the disappearance of Catherine Winters is Henry County's most fascinating mystery. No trace of the little girl has been found since she was last seen at noon on Thursday, March 20th, 1913. Extensive local searches and a nation-wide search failed to locate the child.   If living, Catherine would have celebrated her 100th birthday on February 10, 2004.

The friendly, brown-eyed third grader, left her home on North 16th Street at nine a.m. to sell needles for a church charity. She was last seen about noon, looking at an Easter display in the window of William Siefert's drug store at 16th and Broad. A few yards east of the drug store sat a gypsy caravan of four wagons, which had stopped to water their horses. At this point, only two and one-half blocks from her home, and almost within sight of her front steps, the little girl apparently vanished. She was never seen again.

Authorities immediately suspected the gypsies. Local officials, along with the girl's dentist father, Dr. William Winters, and some of his friends, conducted a 40 hour search in Wayne County that night and into the next day. The gypsy caravan was found outside Economy, Indiana. The little girl was not with them. A reported fifth wagon was never located. It was later concluded that the fifth wagon was a flour wagon from Milton, which was making deliveries on Broad Street the day the little girl disappeared.

On Monday, March 24, four days after her disappearance, the city's business, industrial, and manufacturing elite met in the court room of the Henry County Courthouse and organized a 700 man search for the child. On Tuesday the 25th, amid torrents of rain, the huge search team scoured the city for the child. This massive search produced no clue. Many believed that the downpour of rain, which was the beginning of the disastrous 1913 flood, may have obliterated clues to finding the child.

Authorities were unsuccessful in determining the fate of the little girl. They investigated the gypsy theory, the relative theory and the degenerate theory and could find no leads. Detectives who worked on the case, including those from the famous Pinkerton and Burns agencies, investigated the same theories and came to the same dead end. Detective A. G. Lunt of the Chicago Burns Agency finally gave up in disgust saying, "The Winters case is too deep for the Burns men to fathom." He had even followed the gypsy caravan to the Pennsylvania state line, which so exasperated the gypsy leader that he reportedly offered a $1000 reward to anyone who found Catherine Winters in his caravan.

Dr. Winters seemed devastated and near collapse by his daughter's disappearance, as did Mrs. Winters, the child's stepmother. It was at this time, some said, that Mrs. Winters' hair began to turn white and she lost much weight. The family continued to set a place for Catherine at their large dining room table. Her little brother, Frankie, caught a white cat which he was saving to give his sister when she returned.

Dr. Winters searched area gypsy camps in hopes of finding Catherine. He followed every clue he received, including the many put forth by area psychics and fortune tellers.

In the spring, the doctor went to Chicago in search of his daughter. The Hearst papers emblazoned the story in huge black headlines, city authorities scoured gypsy camps, and the Chicago boy scouts organized a Catherine Winters Search Day. William Randolph Hearst, the newspaper czar, reportedly offered a reward for the child's safe return.

Dr. Winters visited Jane Addams' famous Hull House, where Gertrude Howe Britton, head of the Juvenile Protection Agency, offered him the services of a detective to help in the search for his daughter. The men interviewed relatives of Catherine's mother, the first Mrs. Winters. The doctor returned to New Castle, apparently convinced that Catherine's maternal relatives had nothing to do with her disappearance.

That summer, Dr. and Mrs. Winters tried to seek state aid in the search, from Governor Samuel Ralston. They reportedly met personally with the governor at Indianapolis, but apparently did not receive help.

In the fall, a grand jury investigated the case. The prosecutor questioned many neighbors and friends of the Winters family. Seven-year old Frankie Winters, Catherine's brother, was called to the stand, as well as family members and friends, who had visited the Winters' residence around the time of Catherine's disappearance. This investigation also apparently failed to shed light on the fate of the little girl. By the end of 1913, the trauma and excitement produced by the disappearance had seemingly diminished and New Castle was settled back into a routine existence.

In 1914, it was decided to make the disappearance a national search. Officials from the NEA, an early newsgathering agency, which later became the UPI, came to New Castle to interview the Winters family and to get photographs of the participants in the story. The agency conducted a nationwide campaign in more than 100 papers across the country. Catherine's picture appeared on front pages country-wide. Newspapers reported that the child had been kidnapped by gypsies and offered a five-hundred dollar reward for her safe return. The hunt produced no clues, but it found a home for several young girls.

After the nationwide search, the whirlwind of publicity about the little girl continued. In the spring, a local family, the Gorbetts, wrote a song about the missing child called "Where Did Catherine Winters Go?"

An Indianapolis film company came to New Castle and made a movie of the early search for Catherine. This became known as the Catherine Winters Film. It had its first showing at a packed house in the spring of 1914, at the Grand Theater in New Castle. It was decided to show the movie at other theaters around the state. Dr. and Mrs. Winters traveled with the movie. At each town, before the reel began, a local citizen sang the Catherine Winters Song. Dr. Winters then climbed onto the stage and told the audience about his search for Catherine.

On May 30, 1914, a stunning and unexpected development occurred. The Winters had been in Terre Haute the previous evening showing the film. Upon their return to New Castle, Dr. and Mrs. Winters were arrested and charged, along with their former boarder, William R. Cooper, with conspiracy to commit a felony. Cooper, a one-armed telegrapher with the Big Four Railroad, had been arrested the evening before, after authorities searched the Winters home and apparently found clothing hidden in the basement.

Detective Robert H. Abel, of Indianapolis, charged the three with premeditating to murder Catherine and attempting to burn her body in the furnace of the Winters home. While the Winters were away at Terre Haute, Detective Abel had obtained a search warrant from Mayor J. Leb Watkins, and along with New Castle police, had gone to the Winters home. There, they apparently found, secreted in the basement, a red sweater, (containing apparent burn marks) a red hair ribbon, and a stained man's undershirt.

Abel claimed to have other incriminating evidence and asked prosecutor W.R. Myers to immediately press first degree charges of murder against Mrs. Winters and Cooper. He had concluded that Dr. Winters had no knowledge of his daughter's fate. Prosecutor Myers agreed to file the conspiracy charges, but would not press murder charges, saying there was not sufficient evidence. Detective Abel immediately resigned. "Cowardice and politics have ruined my case." he said angrily.

The conspiracy charges remained on the docket. The trial date was set for July 10, 1914. When the court convened on that day, prosecutor Myers requested that the case be dismissed for lack of evidence. Judge Ed Jackson complied. It was said that a special grand jury would be called to investigate the case, but none ever was.

After the dismissal of the conspiracy charges, life in New Castle returned to normal, although people continued to speculate about the case for years. An elderly New Castle resident recalled that the little girl's disappearance was still a topic of conversation when he came to New Castle in 1922. One life-long resident remembered that Miss May Dorsey, a music teacher, insisted that all her students sing the Catherine Winters song in class.

As the years went by, those connected with the story died. Dr. Winters died in 1940, still saying he believed gypsies took his daughter. Catherine was listed as one of his survivors. Mrs. Byrd Winters, Catherine's stepmother, died in 1953. Catherine's brother, Frankie, moved to California soon after his high school graduation in 1925. He did not return home for the funeral of his father or stepmother. He died in 1955 at the age of 49. William Ross Cooper continued to work for the railroad and died in 1960 at the age of 77.

What really happened to Catherine Winters and where is she today? Detective Abel had been explicit in telling the public his theories. In an affidavit, he accused Mrs. Winters and possibly someone else at the Winters home of conspiring to kill Catherine with a blunt object. He surmised that someone had then tried to burn the child in the furnace, but pulled the body out when they realized that the odor from the burning clothing would drift out into the neighborhood on the spring day. Abel suspected that others connected with the Winters family, helped to spirit the body out of New Castle.

Rumors and gossip about the case has always centered on three main theories,… that a degenerate took the little girl,… that she was stolen by the gypsies,… or that family members were implicated in her disappearance. To this day, none of the speculations have been proved or disproved.

Today, the story has all but faded from everyone's mind. At first, there was a yearly anniversary story, but eventually this stopped. Strangely, for all the attention the story once received, there is no monument or plaque in New Castle to commemorate the memory of the little girl.

Today, the case can still initiate a spirited discussion. Some wonder how a little girl could suddenly disappear on a crowded downtown street on a sunny day without being seen…. or what happened to the clothing found in the Winters basement…. or where the Winters' boarder was, the nine days he was admittedly out of town on sick leave, following the child's disappearance. Yet, the answers to these questions may never be known.

9

Someday, if the child's remains are ever found, DNA technology may help identify her, even if the case is never solved....and it should be remembered...as long as her whereabouts is unknown, the case will never be closed.

Little Ghost Girl

Jan and Howard Brown* had no idea the old white frame house was haunted when they bought it several years ago.

"We started having problems right away." said Jan, a housewife in her thirties.

The first night they moved in, she heard the front door open and close several times. There was no one there. Her husband attributed her fear to being "spooked" because it was an old house.

Later that evening, she took her three year old son Bryan upstairs for a bath. While he was in the tub, he suddenly looked into the darkened outer hallway, which led to the master bedroom, waved excitedly and yelled, "Hi, Violet!" Jan whirled around and looked down the hallway, but saw nothing. Knowing that Bryan's older sister, Violet, was downstairs watching television, Jan quickly wrapped her son in a towel and ran down the steps to the living room.

"Since that time so many things have happened that I can't count them." she said sighing.

The commode flushed without reason, doors slammed suddenly. Once she heard the clang of an old fashioned telephone.

".... And we kept losing things." One day Howard was using a level while doing some remodeling. He laid it on a ledge. When he looked up to get the level, it was gone. They hunted for it three days. They found it lying on the ledge where Howard had originally put it.

They began to see the apparition of a little girl, perhaps the same figure her son had seen that first night in the upstairs hallway. One evening, a sister-in-law was in the foyer about to leave. She had her young son in tow and was unhappy with him because he was dawdling about putting his coat on. She admonished him in a raised voice. At that time she happened to look up. At the top of the stairs stood a young girl, six or eight years old, wearing an

11

old-fashioned dress. The girl swirled quickly around the upstairs banister and went down the long hall towards the master bedroom. Later, another relative saw the girl at the same spot. As the relative started up the stairway to follow her, she was so overcome by the odor of lilacs that she was unable to continue.

One evening, Jan dozed off on the living room sofa. About 3 a.m., she suddenly awakened to see a little girl sitting beside her. Thinking it was her youngest daughter, she said, "Susie, why are you watching television at this time in the morning?" The little girl did not answer, but sat with her hands in her lap, looking straight ahead at the television. Jan looked to the other side and saw her daughter, Susie, sleeping peacefully beside her. Jan turned quickly to look at the other little girl. She was gone.

Both the Browns have heard the little girl at night, walking in the upper hallway. She stops at the end of the long hallway, at the door of their bedroom, and whimpers. Jan sometimes tries to comfort her by saying "Honey, its all right." She says this seems to quiet the girl.

"We have tried to get something on tape. We set up a tripod in the hallway. We haven't seen anything so far." she related.

One Sunday morning, an elderly man came to the door. He had heard they were seeing the apparition of a little girl. He related the story of the death of a little neighbor girl many years ago. Some children had been playing on a nearby railroad track. A train raced through. The little girl was hit and instantly killed. Research revealed that such an incident did happen over fifty years ago, but it occurred several blocks from the Brown's house.

Other unhappy incidents regarding the house and the neighborhood have occurred. A former owner of the house was killed on the railroad tracks while walking to work one morning. Many years before, a little neighbor girl died from burns she received while playing around a bonfire in her back yard. Are any of these events connected with the unusual happenings or the appearance of the little girl? We will probably never know. No evidence has yet been found that a tragedy has befallen a child who lived in the Brown's house.

A visit to the Brown home a few months ago revealed that the paranormal activities had lessened, but Mrs. Brown related that she and her husband felt tired and drained of energy. They talked of putting the house up for sale, but then decided to stay and remodel it. At the time, Howard Brown was busy installing a new door.

Recently, a drive past the house indicated that it was empty. The windows were bare, and there was no sign that anyone ever lived there. Did the activities of the little ghost girl become too overwhelming for the Brown family? Did she go with the Browns when they left…or is she still in the house?

Kearney Cottage at the old New Castle State Hospital, the site of many strange incidents. The building was razed to make way for a prison. It is said that many years ago, a patient was killed in a fall down the stairs. Credit: photo courtesy of Barbara Cross

"… To Those Who Walked These Grounds."

Beneath the flagpole at the New Castle Correctional Facility is a bronze plaque, on which are engraved the words, "Dedicated to those who walked these grounds. 1905-1998." It honors the many hundreds of employees and patients who were part of the group that made up the New Castle State Hospital during its ninety-three year history.

This plaque is almost all that's left of the rows of brick buildings and cottages which once dotted the grounds… cottages with the quaint names of Nightingale and Rose and Adrian.

Across State Road 103 once stood two other large living areas, the north-east and south-east area, which housed the male population of the hospital. On that side were, and still are, ancient Indian mounds which date back to the time of Christ.

Just east of this area, across Blue River and high on a bluff, once stood New Castle's first businessman's club, the Nipp and Tuck. It served as a meeting place for the city's leading businessmen and its chicken dinners were so famous that they are said to be the reason Benjamin Briscoe and J.D. Maxwell decided to build the Maxwell plant here. Northeast of the clubhouse was Nipp's Springs, owned by James Nipp, which served as a an early day picnic area and recreational grounds. Remnants of both sites still exist today.

In 1905, the state bought 1200 acres of rich Blue River Valley land on which to build the Indiana Village for Epileptics, the original name of the hospital. It was to become a self sustaining enterprise. Nothing remains today of the old village farm where the institution grew and harvested its own vegetables and grain and had its own meat- packing house, barns and water storage system.

A rich lore of ghost stories and legends have built up over the years about those who were housed on the grounds and about those who took care of them. There were good times at the "village", but there were also tragedies.

Some still remember the story of the despondent young man who jumped from the water tower after warning officials of his plans...or the man who hung himself in the basement of a cottage because he hadn't heard from his family, (only to receive a letter from them a few days later) ...or the young woman patient, who, against her supervisor's orders, went to the railroad tracks and was killed when a metal projectile, which jutted from the train, struck her in the temple.

Ghostly stories circulated about the eerie laboratory, which for a time housed the morgue, and the brains of deceased patients. These specimans were part of a special epilepsy research study. Each brain was tagged and placed in formaldehyde. Eventually when the study was completed, they were sent to a nearby university.

The Indian mounds were the source of legends about trolls, those ancient, ogre-like creatures, said to appear when Indian remains are disturbed. In 1988, a nurse working at the hospital received a call from an employee to come to the basement of the Administration Building, which then housed extremely disabled patients. When the nurse arrived, the female employee related that she had seen a short, bowed, creature with dangling arms, in the laundry room. She described it as a "troll." The nurse was inclined to laugh and make light of the story until she saw the serious demeanor of the employee.

I remember the incident well, for I was the nurse. This occurred within a year of the time the state replaced an old bridge on 103, which was very near the hospital grounds. During the process, construction had to be stopped because workmen had unearthed an ancient Indian commissary site. Several ancient Indian skeletons had been discovered. Could the sighting of the "troll" by the employee have been connected to the disturbance of the Indian burial site?

If the troll story seems unbelievable, read the account of Edrick Thay in his recent book, "Ghosts of Indiana", in which he tells of the small blue-gowned dwarfs seen at Mounds Park, near Anderson. Thay also relates that, several years ago, Fate magazine published an article about a man who saw these little creatures in Mounds Park in 1927, and spent his life trying to learn more about them. According to an article by David Mannweiler, this park has been placed on the National Haunted Sites list primarily because of the appearance of these little people.

Many other strange occurrences are rumored to have taken place at the old state hospital. Office and administrative staff still talk of the "phantom" office machines. Often they would hear clicking from typewriters and staplers. "Many of us heard them just clicking away." said one former worker. "Even the superintendent knew about it."

Robert Young, now retired, worked at the hospital in 1962 as an attendant supervisor. His office was in the Kearney Building, which had the reputation of being one of the most "haunted" cottages at the hospital. At the time, he worked downstairs and the upstairs was empty.

Young often heard footsteps overhead, doorknobs turned mysteriously, the radio came on by itself, toilets would flush. It appears that eventually, even the security men didn't want to answer the calls from Kearney. "One night we called them and they wouldn't come." Young related. Some believe that the building may have been haunted by the spirit of a young man, who, many years ago, had been killed there when he fell down the stairs.

Today the old hospital grounds and buildings have been replaced by a state prison. Are the ghosts still there? According to a nurse working in the main prison building, they may be.

One evening, not too long ago, she was walking down the main hall on her way to work. Along the long hall are many glass windows. As she passed one of the windows, she saw a reflection of a short, squat person, standing with his arms dangling at his sides. She had the impression that he wanted her to see him. When she got over her shock, she looked at the glass again. He was gone. She hurried on to her work station. She has not seen the apparition again. Was this one of the "trolls", similar to the one seen by the female employee years earlier in the old Administration Building?

According to a nurse who formerly worked there, the prison guards sometimes hear the laughter and crying of children. The area in the main prison building, where many guards work, covers the ground on which, Nightingale Cottage, a unit for developmentally disabled children, once stood. A short distance away is the Barton Building, which was formerly the children's unit. It seems the "ghosts" may not yet be ready to depart.

The Amorous Ghost

The old-fashioned frame house stands on a tree-lined street in one of New Castle's oldest additions. It resembles one of the quaint turn-of-the-century cottages often seen on the cover of "Good Old Days" magazine.

Neighbors say the house has long contained an "amorous ghost" who shows up in the attic and pinches the "bottoms" of those unfortunate enough to venture there. Not many are aware of the house's peculiar tenant, or of its history.

They do know that lately the house has been for sale often. A neighbor man, who not too long ago, helped a new owner move into the house, noted that it had an "unfriendly atmosphere." He also commented that the types of people who have lived there seem rather reclusive and depressed. No one stays long. During the past months, it has been for sale, twice, and for rent, once.

Research may have revealed the reason for the house's "unfriendliness."

Many years ago, a man lived there with his wife. One evening, in a jealous rage, he shot her, and then shot himself in the head. The wife recovered, left him, and later divorced him. The man continued to live in the house. He never recovered from his head wound and died in the house several months later.

Further research revealed that several years before the man died, the wife of a couple he had befriended, poisoned herself in the house, by drinking carbolic acid. Thirty years later, another owner hung herself from a water pipe in the basement. Ironically, a couple then lived in the house for many years without apparent problems.

Does the sinister history of the house explain the recent vacancies? Has the amorous ghost resumed his former haunting activities, or did he ever stop? To find the answer, we may have to wait for the next "for sale" sign.

The Repentant Friend

Sometimes spirits seem to have a special reason for returning to visit the living. This appears to be the case in the following story told by a long-time New Castle resident.

Nettie* and Lois* were childhood friends who went to school together in the hectic war-time years of the 40's. "I really admired Lois." Nettie related, "But as time went by, it became obvious that she felt superior to me. She would say hurtful and demeaning things to me. Her family had money and my family was of modest means." Lois continued to make it clear that she felt socially and economically superior to her friend. In time, the girls grew apart.

The years passed. Lois became ill and was at the point of dying. She asked Nettie to come and see her. Nettie went to see her schoolgirl friend.

"You look so nice." Lois told her. Nettie was surprised for she was unaccustomed to receiving compliments from Lois.

Lois died shortly afterward. Nettie went to the funeral home to see Lois even though she was saddened when she remembered the unkind comments Lois had made to her over the years.

One evening, after Lois' funeral, Nettie was lying in bed. Suddenly, she looked up to see Lois standing beside the rocking chair in her bedroom. Shocked, she sat upright in bed. "Why are you here?" she asked Lois. "Because I was never very nice to you." replied Lois, who then disappeared.

"It's the first and last time such an unusual thing has ever happened to me." Nettie said. She doubted her senses. She was so upset, she told her husband and children. Surprisingly, they believed her, never doubting that such a thing could happen. Lois has never appeared again. Nettie says philosophically, "I guess that was her way of apologizing to me. I still think of her, of course, especially every time I look at that rocking chair."

A photo of Henry Bundy with the Madstone resting on his left hand.
Credit: photo courtesy of Edna Mae McKee and Kelly Ellington

The Bundy Madstone

Henry Bundy, an early New Castle resident, was the proud owner of a healing stone called the Bundy Madstone. It was used to draw poison from animal-bites and other infected lesions. Bundy brought the stone with him to New Castle in 1882. His family acquired it in 1802 from an Indian woman in North Carolina.

It had the prime requirement for a healing stone…it came from the stomach of a deer. The stone, which Bundy called "the little critter", was a pink, wafer-shaped object, one-inch long, one-half inch wide and one-eighth inch thick. Between 1882 and 1907, the year of Bundy's death, New Castle was well-known as the home of this healing stone.

Bundy lived with his family at 2108 Walnut Street. The house still stands today and is a private residence. Newspaper accounts state that hundreds came to the house to have the madstone applied. According to the July 24, 1902 edition of the Courier Times, Fremont Windsor 11, of Sycamore, Indiana, was treated with the stone after being bitten by a dog. The Anderson News reported that Fay Bronnenburg, of Chesterfield, was treated with the stone on June 15, 1904. In November 1912, Harrold Brookshire, of New Castle, was treated for a dog-bite

The stone, after being applied to a wound, would adhere and apparently draw the toxin until it was full, then drop off. Adherence time seemed to be related to the amount of toxin in the system. The record time was said to be three weeks, after it was applied to the wounds of an old soldier, whose system was saturated with poisons from a bullet wound. Apparently, the stone continued to be an effective healer because a steady stream of people continued to visit the house throughout the years.

After Bundy's death, the stone went to his daughter, Mrs. Albert (Huldah) Kendall. From that time on, it has been bequeathed to the favorite child. Today, the owner of the stone is Edna Mae Kendall

McKee, Henry's great-granddaughter. She was interviewed recently in Shelbyville at the home of her granddaughter, Kelly Ellington.

Mrs. McKee and her granddaughter had the stone laid out in a clear plastic, cotton-lined case. Lying beside it were the two penknives which had once been used to clean the wounds of patients who came for treatment. Mrs. McKee explained how the stone had been used. She saw it applied many times by her father, John Kendall, who inherited it after the death of his mother, Huldah Kendall.

"The site of the wound was scratched or opened with the penknife and the stone was applied directly to the open area." she related.

If the stone adhered, it was assumed to be drawing out the poison from the body. When the stone became "full", it dropped from the wound. It would then be cleaned and re-applied to see if it would draw out more liquid. If not, the stone was soaked in milk. "You could see liquid run from the stone." Mrs. McKee related.

She recalls that people used to lodge at the Kendall residence during their treatments. "My grandmother had a big garden and she and my grandfather would fix meals for them." She does not remember if there was a charge for the treatments. "I do know they never turned a needy person away."

She did not remember anyone still living who had received treatment from the stone. She did remember one young man, a neighbor boy, now deceased, who had a troublesome sore on his leg. She laughed as she recalled how much he loved corn. When he came for his treatment, he loudly told her grandmother, Huldah, "I want you to fix me eight ears of corn!" She doesn't remember if he got the corn, but he was cured of his lesion. "Actually," she said, "my great grandfather, Henry, admitted to only one failure in the whole time he used the stone."

After Bundy's death, a controversy arose about the efficacy of the stone. Indiana scientists attacked it as a relic of the days of superstition and witchcraft. Dr. J. W. Hurty, Secretary of the State Board of Health, didn't believe in its powers, calling it a thing of the dark ages. State Geologist, W.S. Blatchley declared that if the stone had any healing powers, it was due to the fact that it allayed the fear in the mind of the victim. Dr. T. Victor Keene, head of the Indiana

Pasteur Institute and an expert on rabies, called the madstone a "fallacy" and regretted that people continued to believe in it.

It was pointed out by others, that the doctors making judgments on the stone knew nothing about madstones except what they had read in encyclopedias or textbooks. They had never seen a treatment, touched, or studied the Bundy madstone or any of the madstones of proven quality, such as the Dyer madstone at Dyer, Indiana or the madstone owned by the Tanner heirs at Milan, Indiana.

"I suppose it is just a relic now." Mrs. McKee said wistfully. But, she still believes in its powers. "I was there many times when my grandparents, Albert and Huldah Kendall, used the stone with beneficial results." she said firmly.

Does she think it would still work? She smiled and replied, "I wouldn't doubt it." She realizes though, that there are faster and more effective cures today.

Mrs. McKee has just given the stone to her granddaughter, Kelly, who plans to keep it under lock and key. Kelly wants to learn more about the history of the stone and intends to keep its legend alive. If she has children, she will, as has always been the family custom, give the stone to them.

The Black Cloud

Cathy Watkins* lives in an old part of New Castle once called Oakland. It was originally a residential development built about 1912 for housing employees who worked in the industrial area near the Maxwell factory.

Her family bought a house in the area in the1930's. It has been in the family for more than sixty years. Recently, they built a new home over the ground where the old one stood. "We used some of the wood from the old house." said Cathy.

One morning, not long ago, Cathy and her sister Janie*, were talking in the new kitchen of the house. Suddenly, a black, cloud-like, apparition began floating into the kitchen from a door nearby. The sisters stood in stunned silence as they watched the cloud float across the kitchen and into the living room. They ran after it and saw it going into the foyer, where it disappeared.

Cathy described the black cloud as elongated and about five foot high. "It was above our heads. It took about a minute for it to cross the kitchen and float into the living room." she related. "We felt a coldness as it passed." Both women intuitively believed the object to be "evil" in nature.

Sometime after this incident, Janie, who also lives in the house, had a frightening experience. She suddenly awakened from a nap feeling very cold. Someone or something very heavy seemed to be holding her down. The pressure lasted approximately one minute before she was able to get up and walk about.

When asked if there had ever been a tragedy in the house, Cathy answered, "My mother died here, but she had a peaceful death." She thinks a relative may have committed suicide in the house many years ago. She doesn't know the history of the dwelling or who owned it before her parents bought it. The family has not experienced any further unusual manifestations. They are puzzled about the cause of the phenomena, but they feel no fear of the house and have no plans to move.

"Our Little Friend."

The snug little bungalow is tucked away on a side street on New Castle's east side. It is a few blocks from the old Hernly School district. Sarah and Randy Owens,* the parents of three small children, bought the house several years ago. Both of the Owens' believe themselves to be practical, objective people. Both lead active lives. Randy is in law enforcement and Sarah is studying for a business degree.

About three years ago, Sarah overheard her two small daughters talking to someone in their bedroom. She related, "Although I knew there was no one else in there with them, I heard them talking to a little boy. I heard his laughter. I saw his shadow on the wall."

When she asked the girls who they were talking to, they replied, "Oh, just our little friend."

As time went by, the girls continued to play and converse with the little boy. Sarah could hear them laughing and giggling together. One day, in a moment of exasperation at something he had said, she told the little fellow, "If you don't behave, you will have to leave." She did not see him again.

Several months passed. One night, she was awakened by someone whispering in her ear, "Megan needs you." She went to her daughter's room and found her feverish and vomiting. The little girl had tried to call out to her mother but had been unable to. Sarah wondered if it was the little boy who warned her.

On another night, she got up to tend to her baby. As she was walking through the living room, she looked up to see the little boy's reflection on the darkened television screen. He was sitting in the recliner. He appeared to be about four years old, and was dressed in a t-shirt, overalls and had an old-fashioned bowel-type haircut. He didn't utter a word, but Sarah believed he was watching her reaction to him.

Today, she no longer hears the conversations between the little boy and her daughters. The girls have grown older and do not seem to remember him. Sarah hasn't seen him lately, but she feels his presence. She does not believe that there is anything evil or menacing about the little boy. "I think he's just lonely and wants someone to play with."

This is a photograph of the Winters home a few months prior to the opening of the Bed and Breakfast in 1994. Credit: author's collection

The House That Spoke

When I first saw the "For Sale" sign on the lawn of the Catherine Winters house, I thought, "Who would ever buy that house?" It had always appeared sinister and depressing... not a house I would ever want to live in. Everyone in town knew the story of Catherine, the little nine- year old girl who had lived there. In the spring of 1913, she suddenly disappeared on a down-town street and was never seen again.

I grew up in the neighborhood and had first heard the story from my mother when I was a little girl. There were various theories of what happened to the child...gypsies...an abductor... her family. The mystery intrigued me. I had recently made the story a project for a college class in Indiana history. Yet, I never suspected that for all my intense involvement in the story, I would ever own the house.

Yet, I found myself drawn to it. Three weeks after seeing the sign, I bought the home. I moved in on June 1, 1988. On move-in day, I entered the hall carrying my beautiful, white Persian cat, Alexander. I went to the bottom of the staircase and looking up into the shadowy stairwell, impishly said, "We're back!" How naïve I was, and what a surprise I had in store.

I had been warned by the former owners that she and her family had observed some mysterious things in the house. I ignored this as I knew myself to be a practical and earthy person, not easily intimidated. I had always believed in "ghosts and spirits", but in a light-hearted way. I had never had a paranormal experience.

I chose the largest room upstairs as my bedroom. It would be the room where I slept for the seven years that I lived in the house. It seemed to have been a master bedroom. It was the first door to the right at the top of the stairs. I never entered that room without feeling a sense of eerie expectancy, a thought that I would see something horrible or that something dire would happen to me at that spot.

The most notable thing about the house was its feeling of oppressiveness. It began the moment I entered the screened-in front porch. It seemed almost as if someone were clinging to me, hugging me, not wanting to let me go. The rooms always seemed so dark, no matter how much sunlight was outside.

I noticed that I never called the house "my home". I always called it, "the Winters home." A few weeks after I moved in, a series of events began which would, one day, lead to my decision to sell the house.

One morning, I happened to look in through the dining room at a leather shoestring that, for some reason, I had placed over the doorknob of the bathroom. It suddenly began to swing back and forth, slowly at first, then faster and faster, until the ends of the shoestring were almost even with the doorknob. I sat mesmerized as the shoestring continued this motion about fifteen minutes. Puzzled, I checked for a breeze or a fan. There was no wind and there were no fans on.

Another time, I was reading at the dining room table. A lamp in the living room suddenly swept from an end table and crashed to the carpet, breaking into several pieces. The plug, which had been securely in the socket, was now lying flung out near the lamp, several feet from the socket. I looked for Alexander, thinking he had toppled the lamp. He was nowhere to be found. My common sense told me that my cat, although he weighed about ten pounds, could not have hit the socket with enough force to cause the lamp to break into that many pieces on a soft carpet.

The basement seemed to be an ominous area. I had decided to keep Alexander's litter-box down there, but I soon learned that this was a part of the house he did not like. One evening, as I sat in the living room talking to a friend, Alexander came up from the basement. He was walking in a slow, slinking manner.

My friend exclaimed, "Look at his face!" My beautiful Persian was barely recognizable. His eyes were slits as he glared at us with an evil look. He passed us and went into another room, seemingly unaware of our presence. I always wondered what he could have encountered down there that made him look and act in such a manner.

The strange phenomena continued. Articles would be moved about or found in areas where I had not placed them. Several times, others, including my daughter and myself, would hear the soft bouncing of a ball in the master bedroom upstairs. I somehow associated this noise with Catherine's younger brother, Frankie, whom I heard had been a mischievous little boy who played pranks on others.

I was becoming slightly alarmed at the unusual occurrences, but I was not yet prepared to admit that the house may be "haunted" or that I had been foolish enough to move into such a house. By this time, I was seriously researching the Catherine Winters story and intended to publish my conclusions about her disappearance from the material I had gathered.

I had interviewed all the known relatives on both sides of Catherine's family and had read extensively on the case. I had talked with many, whose parents and relatives had "first-hand information." about the story. I had also gathered valuable information and pictures while traveling and researching in other states. Only recently, a family relative had loaned me the original 1913 Catherine Winters film, which I made into a video

Yet, I knew that if I wanted to remain in the Winters home, I would have to find a way to relieve the heavy atmosphere there.

I asked a church group to come to the house. They came one evening, and formed a circle in the living room, praying earnestly for the release of negative energies. This helped a few weeks, but gradually the heaviness returned along with the renewal of the strange incidents.

One evening, some friends were visiting. The man's wife and I were in the den, which had originally been Dr. Winters' dental office, and later, Mrs. Winters' sewing room. The husband was in the living room reading a magazine. He later related to another friend that he heard faint strains of music coming from somewhere within the house while he was reading. There had been no music playing.

The most eerie and unexplainable incident occurred one afternoon when my sister-in-law visited. We had been discussing the story of the disappearance, and she wanted to see the attic. We started to ascend the steps to the attic door. I suddenly felt uneasy about going any farther. My sister-in-law, who was in front of me, said teasingly, "Oh, come on!" and started swiftly up the stairs.

At that moment, we heard a doll's cry. It came from a corner of the attic. We looked wide-eyed at one another, as if to confirm that we had both heard the same thing. She turned and swiftly came down the stairs. There had been no doll in the attic. Catherine's doll, which was stored in a closet in my bedroom, had no voice box. I remembered that Mrs. Winters had stored Catherine's doll and buggy in the attic for years, but it had not been in the attic since her death, thirty-five years earlier.

By this time, I was fatigued with the endless chain of unusual happenings. Most of the afternoon and evening, I was out of the house at my job as a nursing supervisor in a state facility. But, when I came home at night, I was again faced with the unexpected…and, I always experienced an inevitable sense of dread as I climbed the stairs and turned to enter the master bedroom. Although nothing ever happened when I turned that corner, I always felt fearful when approaching it.

In a moment of exasperation, I put the house up for sale. Several people came to look at it, but no one made an offer. I decided that redecoration would help. It might brighten the dank and dark atmosphere of the house. I began to think of making it into a Bed and Breakfast, believing that this would add positive energies.

In the spring of 1993, I invited a well-known Indianapolis psychic to visit the house, believing that she might give me some answers. She had a good reputation, had appeared on the Oprah show and other national television shows, as well as being featured in several national books on ghost-lore and psychic phenomena. She had acquired a reputation for ferreting out ghosts and exorcising them.

She agreed to come. When she arrived, I took her on a tour of the house. I did not tell her about the house's history until she had given me her psychic impressions. I don't believe she had ever been to New Castle. I'm sure she had never heard of Catherine Winters or her disappearance.

She allowed me to tape her comments. She concluded that an upstairs bedroom, an area in the upstairs hall, the basement and the dining room were places of special oppression.

At an upstairs bedroom, she stopped and touched the door before she entered. "Terrible things have happened here." she said gravely. She did not elaborate. This was a room that I surmised, by process of elimination, had belonged to Catherine or Frankie.

Suddenly, she paused in the upper hallway, near the master bedroom, close to the area where I always dreaded to turn the corner. She closed her eyes and pursed her lips. A look of distress came over her features. "I feel someone is slapping my hands over and over. They just keep doing it. It's very painful."

Could someone have ever been punished in this manner and at this spot? Is this why I felt the dread every time I reached the top of the stairs and started to go into the master bedroom?

The psychic reported that the basement was heavy with "negative energy". She had sensed the presence of an older man, who, she said, was almost like a "prisoner", and a short, black-haired woman, filled with anger. The psychic was among several who found the basement an unpleasant place to be.

The former owners had reported eerie experiences in the basement. They had felt the presence of a man watching as they showered. I always felt "watched" when I was down there. The most sinister connection in the basement, though, had to be the rumor that someone had attempted to burn the little girl in the furnace that sat just to the right of the stairway.

In the dining room, the psychic went to an area on the west side of the room, in front of the entrance to the bathroom. There, she felt a "cold spot." "I feel something may have happened here."

I knew that in the Winters era, the dining room table once sat near this spot, and where the bathroom door now was, had once been Catherine's favorite window seat. It was alleged, in my research, that in this room, very near this spot, Catherine had been struck on the head with something blunt. The psychic had no knowledge of this as she had never heard the story.

After the psychic completed the tour of the house, I told her the story of the disappearance. She believed that Catherine had been killed in the house and that some part of her might still be here or on the premises. She asked suddenly, "Have you ever thought of x-raying the walls?"

She told me that I would be selling the house and moving on to other things. I was shocked and told her, "No, I don't intend to sell, I'm going to make it into a Bed and Breakfast. She replied calmly, "Well, you may, but you're still going to sell. You are completing a cycle. You will be writing something about this story."

"I'm not a writer." I quickly replied. "Oh yes you are, my dear, and you will find that out." she said confidently.

I was definitely impressed with details she gave me about the members of the Winters family. I already knew much about the family from interviews and there was no way she could have known these details except by paranormal means. They were details I had never told anyone and they had not been published anywhere.

Before she left, she performed a rite somewhat like the church members had, directing the offending "entities" to go home to God. Her efforts cleared the atmosphere for a few months, but the strange happenings began again.

I began making plans to move ahead with the redecoration of the house. I had not really believed the psychic when she told me I would be selling the house. By early 1994, much of the painting, papering and carpet-laying were complete. I had been lucky in getting a talented, local decorator and other local people to help me.

The house began to resemble a very pretty 1912 replica of what it once was. The outside of the house had been changed earlier. A downstairs bathroom, a small room at the back and a back deck had been added by the former owners. The outside, which had been covered with ugly gray shingles, had been improved with a coat of white paint. The original front porch had long ago been torn off and replaced by a screened-in porch. My white wicker porch furniture added a classic touch and colorful flower beds made the outside attractive. I added a blue and white Bed and Breakfast sign with a logo of Catherine.

I began to feel good about the project. One evening, after a hard day's work, I trudged up the stairs to the master bedroom. At the top of the stairs, I turned and looked down at the bottom of the steps. Alexander sat looking up at me. I said "Come on up Alex, its time for bed." He continued to look up at me.

I went to bed and slept soundly. The next morning, a workday, I hurried down to eat breakfast and get ready for work. I suddenly thought with a start, "I haven't seen Alex this morning." I called him, but he did not come. I checked the downstairs and the basement, then went back up to recheck the master bedroom.

As I entered the room, I saw him lying with his face toward a corner of the bedroom, his eyes half open. He was cold and stiff. Like a child, I began to cry and leaned down and hugged him, calling his name. I couldn't understand it. He seemed fine the evening before. I remembered how he had rolled playfully on his back in the living room, as I sat in the corner of the room that had been Dr. Winters' favorite sitting area.

After Alexander died, I was more determined than ever to complete my plans. I wondered if his death was connected with the unusual things going on in the house. It was a horrible thought to contemplate. Had I, in any way, been the cause of my beloved pet's death?

I was even more determined to finish the project. In October, 1994, I was ready to open the Bed and Breakfast. I scheduled an open house, which with the help of my family and friends, was very successful.

I was discouraged, though, when several people told me that day, they felt there was something strange about the house. I did not ask them for an explanation. I wasn't sure whether they saw things or felt things. That evening, I had a caterer bring in food for those who had helped with the open house.

The decorator, Jill Morris, and her husband, Mike, playfully asked if a few people could see the basement. I assumed they wanted to see the "dug out areas" made years ago when authorities searched for Catherine's body…..or perhaps they wanted to look at the furnace, rumored to be the original one.

Jill and Mike and several others descended the basement stairs and in a few minutes hurried back up the stairs laughing. My daughter and I were sitting in the living room and heard the basement door slam loudly. As they came into the room, they still seemed amused. I didn't question them. I didn't know until recently, when Mike told me, that they weren't the ones to slam the door. Mike related that the last person to leave the basement started to shut the door. The knob was jerked from their hand and the door was slammed by someone or something unseen.

The Bed and Breakfast did reasonably well, business was slow, but I believed things would improve. However, as time went by, I became listless and unhappy. I believe now that living in the house caused me to fall into a state of deep depression without realizing it.

The sale of the house came so quickly, I hardly realized it happened. I had thought of selling it, but was undecided. One morning, I was eating breakfast in a local restaurant and thumbing through the latest realtor's magazine. A realtor came to my table and handed me her business card. In less than a week, she found a buyer for me. I gave the new owners a disclosure statement about the history of the house. They did not seem to mind and told me they already knew about the house.

I moved out in June, 1995. The psychic had been right. I did leave the house (about two years after she told me I would) and I am writing about it, as she said I would.

Sometimes, I wonder if I just imagined the things that happened there. But, I know that they did happen. Numerous other people saw the phenomena also.

I did not complete the book I started to write about the little girl's disappearance. Perhaps, someday, I will. I still wonder what happened to her. I find it strange that I never once felt her presence in the house the whole time I lived there. I know there may be "others" there, who are troubled souls, but I believe the spirit of Catherine Winters is at rest.

The Haunted Apartment

Several years ago, Patty Jackson* and her two daughters, Pam* and Judy*, moved into an apartment in an old building in New Castle's business district. They lived there peacefully for a time. One night, they experienced a series of frightening events which made them doubt their senses.

The apartment was small and they had to share a bedroom. One evening, as they retired, Pam, who was nine at the time, was about to doze off for the night. As she began to close her eyes, she thought she saw the filmy outline of a woman bending over the kitchen sink.

About 2 a.m., Patty was awakened by the sound of running water. She got up to check the kitchen area and found water droplets in the sink, as if someone had recently turned the faucet on. She knew the sink had been dry when she went to bed. She opened the refrigerator door to get a bottle of milk to feed her youngest daughter, Judy, who was a few months old.

She was startled to see that the milk bottle was almost empty, although she clearly remembered that it contained considerably more milk when she went to bed. When she returned to the bedroom to get the baby's bottle to fill it, the bottle was gone.

Meanwhile, Pam awakened in time to see a bright, glowing ball of light sweep into the bedroom. It hovered near the top of her head, and began to travel down her forehead and on down her body. She remembers she felt paralyzed during the time the orb made contact with her. It suddenly zipped forward through the air and disappeared under her mother's bed.

Patty and Pam, now wide awake and terrified, spent the remainder of the night sitting up with all the lights on. The baby slept peacefully through it all. The Jacksons moved from the apartment as soon as they could arrange it. Before leaving, Patty told a lady in a neighboring apartment of the experience. "Why honey," the neighbor exclaimed when she heard the story, "Didn't you know this used to be a funeral home?"

Research bore out the fact that the building had, indeed, been an undertaking parlor for many years.

The baby's bottle was never found and mother and daughter still wonder what the ghostly orb of light meant and why anyone would have wanted the baby's bottle or the milk. Both of them still have a vivid memory of the experience and remember how frightened they were.

The Spectre Nurse and the Man in Black

Hospitals and nursing homes are known for having those ghostly entities, sometimes called "death angels", whose duty seems to be to come for a dying patient, or warn that a death is near. Two entities rumored to "haunt" the cluster of nursing homes in the north end of town, are a nurse dressed in white, and a man dressed in black.

One former employee, Keith Burkman, R.N., used to be an orderly in one of these nursing homes several years ago. He remembers, "Whenever a patient's condition worsened, we often saw the dark shadow of a man enter the patient's room. When we checked, we always found the patient in a dying state." He added, "Not only this … if we saw a woman in white enter a room, we knew that the patient would already be dead." According to Burkman, this happened without fail.

The story goes that the first appearance of the woman in white began when a nurse who worked at one of the nursing homes was killed in an automobile accident. After this, the female in white began to make her appearance in the rooms of deceased patients.

"At first we thought the woman in white was our staff nurse, Willie*, because she always wore her white nursing uniform, white hat, and nursing shoes." says Burkman, "But when we checked, we always found Willie at her work station." That's when the staff started making rounds in pairs. Burkman worked at the nursing home five years and states confidently that the phenomena of the nurse in white occurred at least once a month the entire time he worked there.

"We were always feeling cold spots and bumping into things that we could not see.", he related. Dianne Mercer-Elmore, R.N., who worked at the same nursing home several years ago, also says she often felt the cold spots, especially when she attended a dying patient. Burkman stated that while he was employed there, he worked with four or five female aides, and they were all aware of the happenings, but no one talked about it.

The ghostly visitations apparently continue to this day. The man in black and the nurse in white are still encountered. An aide at one of the neighboring nursing homes recently told of seeing a black shadowy figure pass by one evening when she was in the break room. Another time she saw feet under the door of a unit she was about to enter. The unit contained only wheelchair patients who could not walk.

According to the aide, the staff is told of the apparitions by the patients themselves. She heard one patient tell another, "I saw that man in black last night." Another, asked her, "Did you see that pretty woman in white over there?" A patient in a dying state was heard to cry out, at no one in particular, "Oh sir, please come back, don't leave me."

Rumor has it that former patients, who have died, sometimes return to annoy or frighten the staff by turning on the showers, playing with the call lights or holding the doors shut to prevent staff from leaving or entering a room.

Since death and tragedy is an integral part of nursing home life, it's likely that stories about these two "death angels" will continue to be told for a long time to come.

The Tavern Ghost

Back in the busy days of the Chrysler, the south end of town was dotted with numerous taverns. One of these, no longer in existence, and only a stone's throw from the Chrysler, had it's beginnings in the 1930's. It was like most taverns around factories....smoky, noisy, and always packed with patrons. The difference with this tavern was that it harbored an unhappy male ghost. According to an employee who once worked there, the ghost was angry, often slammed doors, and moved glasses and ashtrays around on the bar.

As soon as the employee came to work, the ghost began his nightly routine of slamming and throwing. Sometimes, when he was in a more playful mood, he would wait until a patron entered the restroom, and then hold the door so they couldn't get out.

The ghost was never seen, but his presence was felt everywhere..... at the bar, in the balcony, in the bathrooms. He left "cold spots" in certain areas. Other patrons were aware of this, but apparently became accustomed to his antics.

Eventually, the tavern was destroyed by fire. Apparently, the unhappy spirit left, for his presence was no longer felt.

Who was he? What was the cause of his anger? Although it is not known for certain, the employee believes he may have been a former patron who suffered some wrong at the tavern. Perhaps he was barred from entering, or injured in a fight, or experienced some other unhappy circumstance.

Monkey Jack Bridge today. Legends and ghostly stories still exist about the old bridge and the lane leading up to it.

Monkey Jack Bridge

For many years, this rural lane and bridge has been rumored to be haunted. The lane, now closed off by an iron bar, lies just east of Greensboro. It runs north and south and was once used as a short cut to the Spiceland Pike. The small, steel sided bridge, which spans Big Blue River, was built in 1910. Its wooden floor has disintegrated and the river can be seen between the planks. Someone set fire to it a number of years ago. Eventually, the road was closed to protect the public.

Two legends are connected with this lane and bridge. In the first legend, a young couple parked in the lane near the bridge, one evening. The car's radio announced that a killer with an artificial hook-hand had just escaped from a nearby asylum. Becoming frightened, the couple sped off. The next morning, an artificial hook was found dangling from the car's door-handle.

In the second legend, a young couple ran out of gas near the bridge. The boy started for help, telling his girlfriend to keep the car doors locked and the windows rolled up. As his girlfriend drifted off to sleep, she heard something scraping back and forth on the roof of the car. She was awakened early next morning when a state trooper knocked on the car's window. As she emerged from the car, she looked upward, although the trooper had warned her not to. She saw the body of her boyfriend hanging from a tree, his body swaying back and forth, his feet touching the car's roof.

No one seems to know how or when these legends began, or if there are known facts which indicate such incidents happened. Certainly, there were state institutions nearby, ... the New Castle State Hospital, and the Richmond State Hospital.

In the forties, a dangerous psychopath and killer escaped from an Indiana jail and was said to be in the New Castle area for a time, but this report later proved false. There had been a number of escapees from the local jails and other institutions, both here and in nearby areas, but none fit the circumstances of the legends. No person is known to have hanged himself near the bridge area in recent times.

Neighbors and locals tend to discount the legends. A farmer, who has tilled the ground in the area for years, says he has never seen or heard anything. Long-time neighbors remember the bridge and lane fondly as a place where teens used to party. They often danced in the headlights of their cars. Some of the more mischievous would shine their car spotlights on couples who parked in the lane. Others remember the lane as a place to pick raspberries.

Some suggested the hanging man legend may have originated in the seventies or eighties, when it was rumored that cults practiced witchcraft in the area. They say the cult killed a calf and hung it up near the bridge. There were also reports of coyotes and coy-dogs, whose howls resemble a woman's scream. Could this be the source of the eerie, high pitched screams that some say are heard there at night?

According to stories in area newspapers of the eighties, witchcraft may have indeed been practiced in the woods and abandoned buildings of the area. The witchcraft explanation is reinforced by a woman who lived near Monkey-Jack Bridge at the time of the reported satanic rituals. She related, "Beyond the bridge (south) was a curve and just beyond that, a grove of trees. People used to go back in that grove and kill animals. We could hear them screaming. It was terrible. Once we found a mutilated cat nearby."

Does this information make the legends obsolete? Have the remains of slaughtered animals or the howl of coy-dogs been the source of the legends? Is this peaceful, pastoral lane, with gentle cows grazing contentedly in adjoining pastures, really haunted?

Frightening stories are still being told about the bridge and the lane. At least one former Greensboro resident swears that a Greensboro bus driver once saw a man hanging from a tree over the bridge, in daylight hours. The experience was so frightening that he never talked about it to anyone.

A nearby resident tells the story that one night, she and her high school friends were sitting on the edge of the bridge, when suddenly, they saw car headlights moving toward them from the lane. As the teens sat frozen, fearing they were going to be struck, the lights zoomed silently past them, went through the bridge and disappeared. She said, "That was the last time I ever went down there."

A young woman related that some of her friends recently visited Monkey Jack Bridge after dark and were frightened by horrible screams coming from somewhere in the area.

"It's at night that you hear all the really scary stuff." she said.

It is one thing to go down to Monkey Jack Bridge in daylight hours, but would anyone go down there at night? Any volunteers?

Jonathan Bond and the Three Spirits. Bond built the Mt. Lawn mansion. His activities in the séance room may be responsible for many of the eerie tales about the mansion. Credit: Biographical Memoirs of Henry County. 1902. B.F. Bowen. Reprint 1978, The Bookmark. Knightstown, Indiana.

Mt. Lawn Mansion

A well-known Henry County haunt was the old Jonathan K. Bond mansion, north of Greensboro, on the grounds of the Mt. Lawn Race Track. Bond, a Quaker turned Spiritualist, built the house in 1874.

The house's ominous reputation may have begun when Bond built a windowless séance room on the second floor of the nine room house. It was rumored that after the death of his wife, he used the séance room in an attempt to contact her spirit. There is no record of whether he was successful, but a photograph in the 1902 edition of The Biographical Memoirs of Henry County pictures Bond surrounded by three spirits, two of whom are said to be his mother and father.

After Bond died in 1905, the house went through a series of owners and tenants. Over the years, the house with the arched windows and gothic look, acquired a sinister reputation.

Judy Bowling-Hyatt, who lived in the mansion with her family for seven years, described the strange experiences she encountered there.

"One night I was asleep in my room," said Hyatt, "and I thought my Mom had come in and woke me up...because somebody shook me." But it wasn't her mother. When she looked up, the door was standing open. No one was there.

Some of Hyatt's belongings disappeared. "Pictures that were valuable to me, disappeared...things would be moved around in my bedroom." she related. "The atmosphere in the house was heavy." related Hyatt. "You could feel the spirits there, you felt as if they were sitting in the room with you."

The kitchen was a source of unusual activity. Her mother related, "I'd line things all up to fix a meal. Next morning, they would be scrambled in the cabinets." One day, Hyatt was alone in the living room. She heard a noise in the kitchen. "I thought it was my Dad coming in from work. When I walked in there, the kitchen was empty but you could hear everything (in the cabinets) moving…"

Lights would come on. Lights would go out. Doors would open, but no one appeared. Once, she heard footsteps walking up from the basement and saw the doorknob turn. There was no one there.

She and other family members say they felt the presence of a loving couple. "I got the impression that they loved each other, but that he worshiped her, that she was… like his possession." related Hyatt. Once she thought she saw a glimpse of them in the kitchen.

Hyatt sensed the presence of the woman in the upstairs area of the portico, at the front of the house (which faced the south and overlooked what is now the Mt Lawn racetrack.) Hyatt felt compelled to go out onto the balcony, even though she had always been afraid of heights. The door was sealed but she worked and finally pried it open. Hyatt would then sit and gaze out over the track and fields for long periods of time.

The family moved from the old house in 1972. Both Hyatt and her mother were saddened to leave the mansion. Hyatt's mother commented, "That house loved people, it seemed to enfold you. The more we fixed it up, the more it loved us."

After Hyatt's family left, the house began to deteriorate again. During the 1980's, it was used as a meeting place for teens using drugs and for cult activities.

In the fall of 2003, the crumbling ruins of the old mansion were torn down and a modern dwelling built, nearby. Was the couple that Hyatt saw, Jonathan Bond and his wife? Will the razing of the old house end the legend of Mt Lawn Mansion and the ghostly couple? Time will tell.

Monument of the murdered Mollie Starbuck and her baby girl at the Greensboro Cemetery.

Molly and her Baby

At the north end of the Greensboro Cemetery sits a small monument with the inscription, "Molly and her Baby." The story behind this inscription describes one of the most tragic and mysterious murders ever to occur in Henry County.

Molly Starbuck and her infant daughter were murdered on their farm near Greensboro, on the night of July 9, 1904. That evening, Molly was doing the supper dishes in the kitchen of their farm home. Her three-month-old daughter, Beulah, was sleeping in a crib in another room. Her husband, Will, and their five year old daughter, Olive, had gone into Greensboro to shop. Suddenly, Molly heard someone tampering with the screen in the kitchen window.

When her husband returned, Molly and the baby were not in the house. Will heard cries coming from a grove about one-quarter of a mile south of the house. He bolted out of the house, running toward the direction of the cries. He found Molly in an old abandoned cattle well. She was standing in the water, crying and jabbering hysterically. The baby had been thrown into the well and was hanging head-down, by her dress, with her face in the water.

Molly died at 3.a.m. Monday morning, July 11, unable to identify her killer or killers. The coroner's report listed acute lung congestion as the cause of death. Until she died, Molly babbled incoherently about the intruder or intruders and at one point told her doctor that "some men" had taken her out through the kitchen window.

Neighbor women were called to the Starbuck residence to help prepare the bodies for burial. Molly and her baby were placed in a single white casket. The funeral was held at the Friends Church on Mill Street, which still stands today. A crowd of two thousand jammed the church and grounds. A cortege carried mother and daughter down Mill Street the short distance to the Starbuck family gravesite.

The tragedy created intense interest in the county and the state. The morning after Molly and her child were found, the Courier reported that a crowd of thousands milled about the farm and around the house and the abandoned well. People wondered who would want to kill gentle Molly and her helpless infant. Some believed intruders might have been searching for money that Will had recently received from the sale of farm goods.

From the beginning, authorities suspected more than one man, although suspicion centered on a Greensboro resident, twenty-two-year old Ollie Haley Gipe. He had acted in a suspicious manner, immediately asking questions and making comments about the murder.

Police sent for the well-known, Dayton, Ohio bloodhounds, who tracked a scent to a point just south of Greensboro, on the old Knightstown road. Someone remembered seeing a wagon with three men stopped there shortly before the murder. The men were never identified.

Although several men were questioned and several were even arrested or held temporarily, Gipe was the only one to go to trial. He was first tried in Henry County, where he was convicted of manslaughter and sentenced to, from two-to-twenty years in prison. He won a retrial and the case was re-tried in Rush County. The same verdict was returned. He served four years in the Jeffersonville Reformatory and was released in May, 1909. He relocated at Indianapolis where he died in 1952 at the age of sixty-eight.

The main consensus seemed to be that apparently no one, including the authorities, thought Gipe was guilty of the actual crime.... that he was somehow implicated, but covered-up for the real murderer. Some alleged that Gipe's father was the real culprit. Newspapers hinted at one time, that the elder Gipe would soon be arrested, but this never happened. Will Starbuck was even questioned by the authorities. Four other men were temporarily held for questioning in the murder.

Will Starbuck did not stay another night in his home after Molly's death. He and his little daughter, Olive, moved from the farm and went to live with his father.

Very few people alive today remember the murder of Molly and Beulah. The old Starbuck house still stands and is a private residence. The beautiful, remodeled home and its' peaceful surroundings belie the fact that such a terrible tragedy took place there.

Which Way to Mooreland?

A few years ago, one of the caretakers at a Prairie township cemetery had an eerie experience. It was getting dark and he was in the center of the cemetery cutting weeds. Suddenly, he became aware he was not alone. He felt a touch on his back. He swirled around to see the shadowy figure of a woman standing about fifteen feet away.

"Do you know the way to Mooreland?" she asked. He gave her directions and turned back to his work. With a start, he realized he had not seen a car or headlights, nor had he heard any noise whatsoever while the woman was there. He hurried to look up and down the road, but saw no one.

To this day, he can't figure who the woman was or how she was able to appear and leave so quickly. He knows it was the most chilling experience he has had at the cemetery in all the years he has worked there. He said, "If there ever was a time when I saw a ghost, I believe that was it."

Death Car

Some years ago, the relative of a Henry County resident bought a classic automobile. He stored it in a garage in Prairie Township, intending to restore it. It had been wrecked, but was only slightly damaged. There was only one drawback. A young woman had been killed in the car when it wrecked. Most people would be afraid to buy such a car, but the new owner did not seem to mind.

According to his relative, nothing seemed to go right after the man bought the car. It seemed as though family problems increased and there was more sickness in the family. "We all thought the car was spooky. It gave me the creeps." she said.

Several years went by. The owner of the car never got around to restoring it. One cold winter night, he went into his bedroom, closed the door and shot himself. Today the relative firmly believes the family's troubles began when the man bought the car. After his death, the car was easily sold at an auction. Even the gun, with which the man shot himself, was bought by a neighbor. No one knows where the car or the gun is today. It is hoped that their new owners had better luck than their former one.

The Bangs Sisters' cottage on the grounds of Camp Chesterfield. Now privately owned. The Bangs sisters did many spirit portraits in this house and on the lawn outside.   Credit: Photo printed with permission of the Board of Trustees of Camp Chesterfield.

John Payne's Spirit Photograph

Most people have never seen spirit photographs, those eerie portraits or photographic reproductions of persons who have died. They appear spontaneously without the aid of human hands. Sometimes, they are referred to as "precipitated portraits" and can be accomplished by only the most gifted mediums. May and Lizzie Bangs, early-day Chicago mediums, who spent their summers at their cottage at Camp Chesterfield, were experts at such portraits.

John Payne Jr., of Henry County, engaged the Bangs sisters to do a precipitated portrait of his father, John, who had been dead fourteen years. This would be hard to believe if it were not for the New Castle Democrat's published account of John Payne Jr.'s words describing the event. The younger Payne sent a statement to the newspaper on Friday, August 25, 1905, attesting that he and two other local people watched as they saw his father's image appear on a canvas held by the Bangs sisters. His account follows:

"It was made in the day time in an ordinary room that was not darkened. The frame containing the canvas sat on a stand before the window. Mrs. Charles Payne and Mrs. John Weesner, who do not believe in spiritualism, were with me and we sat within five feet of the picture. The two Bangs sisters, the mediums through whom the likeness was produced, sat on either side of the table and supported the frame, each with one hand. No brushes, paint, crayon or other substance of any kind was used as far as we could tell, and it was light enough to have seen a pin on the table. The sisters had never seen nor heard of my father, nor a photograph or likeness of him. All they asked was that I fix his features in my mind. The picture was not made in spots or (a) little at a time. At first it was a faint shadow, then a wave appeared to sweep across the canvas and the likeness became plainer. It was a good deal like a sunrise- got brighter and brighter until it was perfectly plain and every feature visible. Until the picture was completed the eyes were closed and then they opened all at once like a person awakening. It did not take more than a half hour and is the best picture of my father we ever had. I do not pretend to say how it was done, simply that the picture was produced before our eyes without the mediums having ever seen a photograph or other copy."

The portrait is thought to have been made at the camp on Friday, August 18, 1905. On Thursday, August 24, 1905, the New Castle Courier announced that the spirit portrait of John Payne was on display at the Citizens State Bank and was viewed by more than one hundred people. Payne had once been director of the bank. The newspaper commented that the portrait was not known to have been done by any mechanical means and the picture seemingly produced itself. Unfortunately, no one seems to know where John Payne's spirit portrait is today.

The Bangs sisters continued their artwork at Camp Chesterfield. They called their business "phenomenal psychics." They could give no explanation why they could do the portraits. Their business cards read, "portraits of departed friends a specialty." The house where they lived and where they often did the portraits, still stands within the camp, and is privately owned. Today, twenty-five spirit portraits done by the Bangs sisters are on display at the J.E. Hett Art Gallery, within the camp grounds.

The Charles Dayton Morgan Mansion, Knightstown, which later became known as the "Pest House" after it served as an infirmary for those suffering from smallpox in the 1902 epidemic. Privately owned.

The Lady in Black

The sixteen-room, brick mansion, known as the "Pest House", has long had a sinister reputation in local ghost-lore. It sits high on a hill, east of Knightstown. Nothing seems to eradicate its reputation of being a "haunted house." Certainly it looks the part, with its mansard roof and high tower, reminiscent of an old horror film.

It first gained an ominous reputation in 1902, when the smallpox epidemic invaded Knightstown. The city bought the mansion from its original owner, banker Charles Dayton Morgan, to use as a hospital for victims of smallpox. The epidemic lasted only six weeks. There were fourteen deaths, and only seven of the dead had been patients at the mansion. Yet, the house has continued to carry the distasteful name of "Pest House."

The public apparently reasoned that the house would be forever contaminated by the dreaded disease. Many thought that some of the infected bodies were buried on the grounds. Research indicates there may be reason for this assumption. Public record bears out the fact that most of the victims were buried in local and area cemeteries. Yet, apparently, there are several victims whose actual resting place is not officially recorded.

To add to the unsavory legend, bones were allegedly found while the grounds were being bulldozed for new construction in the 1970's. No one today seems to remember this, although newspaper accounts have mentioned it.

The fact that the mansion was a small pox hospital isn't the only thing that gave it an eerie reputation. As the house went through a series of owners and long periods of vacancies, rumors of apparitions and poltergeist activity began to circulate. It was said that furniture moved about during the night. The ghost of a former female resident was reportedly seen. The mansion was vandalized many times, windows were broken and parts of the interior were destroyed. A story circulated that there was a sealed room where instruments, used in treating smallpox victims, were stored. Several owners have looked unsuccessfully for this hidden room, although it is said that an underground tunnel leading to a nearby house, has been located.

Through the years, many teens have paid a visit to the old house, hoping to see ghosts or experience other frightening adventures. To one "uninvited visitor", the mansion was anything but welcoming. Rick Sweigart, of New Castle, remembers that, as a teen, he and several of his school buddies went through the house during one of its unoccupied periods in the 1960's.

The tour was uneventful until the boys decided to venture out onto a small roof at the back of the house. Someone happened to glance at the driveway where their car was parked. The automobile suddenly began to roll forward. One of the boys jumped ten feet to the ground, ran to the car, quickly hopped in and jammed on the brake.

Although no one was hurt, the group thought it strange that after fifteen minutes of sitting securely, the car began rolling down the driveway at that particular moment. Although this could be called a minor incident, Sweigart recalls that it unnerved him enough that this was his last trip to the old mansion.

For many years, the house changed owners often. Finally, in the late seventies, a family bought the mansion, remodeled and redecorated it and lived there for many years.

One would expect this to be the end of the ghost stories. But after the house was sold to its present owners in 1993, the former owner wrote a series of articles in which she related strange and unexplainable occurrences at the mansion.

She sometimes heard knocks on the bedroom ceiling at night. Surprisingly, when she checked, something was always amiss. The coffee pot was still plugged in, a light was still on, one of the children needed attention.....

During remodeling, one of the workers swore someone hurled a board at him from an upstairs window, even though the owner took him upstairs and showed them the window was sealed.

One evening, when she was visiting in another state, her son called her to make sure she was still away. He related that when he awoke from a nap, a small table fan had been turned away from his face, as if to protect him from too much air, and the dishes on which he had eaten a small snack, had been cleared away.

But, the most chilling and intriguing of her accounts was the story of the Lady in Black. According to the owner, a group of women from Knightstown called at the mansion, one day, hoping for a tour. A lady wearing a long, black dress opened the door. She told them the owner wasn't home. The women left puzzled. They saw a car in the driveway, and they heard someone moving about in the house.

Later, one of the ladies told the owner of the incident. The owner wondered who had answered the door, for she knew she had been home the morning the ladies called. Not long after, the owner got her first glimpse of the Lady in Black as she scampered through a door at the mansion. The owner insists the lady laughed when she realized she had been seen.

After living there seventeen years, the family moved away. The children were now young adults and the house had become too much to maintain. The owner emphasized that she had been sorry to go, and that the presences she felt in the mansion were protective, rather than frightening.

The new owners prefer to call the mansion, Thornhill. They find that living in the house is a positive experience. They attribute things they sometimes think they see or hear to the fact that the mansion is big, and that it is on a hill where there is draft and wind. The wife reportedly said, "We have heard all of the stories and it is amazing that so many people really believe there's something going on at the house."

Still, stories continue to circulate, and the house has an ominous history which may make it difficult to rid it of its sinister reputation. Even if it isn't haunted, it seems to be a place that people love to believe is haunted.

The 1890 Queen Anne style mansion in Knightstown where the mystery woman, Skara Brae, lived for many years.

Who Was Skara Brae?

For thirty years, she was Knightstown's mystery woman. She lived in one room of her seventeen-room, Queen Anne style mansion, at the corner of Jefferson and Brown Streets.

No one knew her real name. She chose the name Skara Brae, which was really the name of an old Scottish settlement. No one knew about her former life or what enticed her to come to Knightstown. She reportedly worked for a doctor. It was rumored she had once been married. Someone said she had children in Indianapolis, but no one ever saw them.

She lived sequestered in the old 1890's mansion, which a reporter compared to the old house in "It's a Wonderful Life." When she died in October, 2002, the house was neglected, the windows broken, the paint faded and scaly. However, it must have once been a beautiful home. It is listed as an outstanding historical site by the Indiana Landmarks Foundation because of its unique architectural style.

Skara was reportedly kind to her few friends. Due to her reclusive ways, when she died, she wasn't found for several days. Her eight-line obituary listed no survivors. A small group, consisting of a local couple, two friends, the cemetery secretary, and a minister, attended the graveside services. Someone later provided money for a cement foundation and there are plans to erect a stone.

It has been said that Skara's house "contained activity". In paranormal terms, this means it might be "haunted." It is certain that Skara would never have mentioned if she had seen anything unusual in the house. A couple recently bought the old mansion and plans to restore it to its original splendor. One wonders if Skara will be around to oversee the new owners' renovations and perhaps give her approval.

A Dream of Death

Mrs. Charles Midkiff, of Knightstown, was preparing for bed. It was Friday, December 13, 1912. It had been an uneventful day for the family.

Her father, Robert Gilson, who lived a short distance away, also apparently had a usual day. Gilson, 70, a Rush County farmer, had moved to Knightstown with his wife, a few years before.

About 4 a.m., Mrs. Midkiff had a dream in which she saw her father very pale and unable to speak. On Saturday morning, when Gilson did not come down for breakfast, the family thought nothing of it, and did not go to awaken him. However, as time passed, Mrs. Gilson became alarmed and entered his room to find him dead. It was thought that he died about the same time his daughter had the dream in which she saw him in distress.

In addition to the fact that his daughter apparently had a precognitive dream about her father's death, Friday the 13th, notorious for being an unlucky day, had been Gilson's last full day on earth.

Huddleston, New Castle, Ind.
Argolda Adams Kiplinger, circa 1895.
Credit: Photograph courtesy of Donna Tauber and Barbara Meade.

Argolda Adams Kiplinger, Lewisville Medium

Argolda Kiplinger, of Lewisville, was a special woman with special powers. Although she had no formal training as a medium, she could see and hear things others could not.

Anybody who knew Argolda knew of her special abilities. "The old-timers at Lewisville could tell you about her." said Barbara Meade, her granddaughter, who was raised by Argolda and her husband Ben Kiplinger. Barbara, who with her husband Don, owns "Country Memories", a florist shop at Spiceland, spoke affectionately of the woman who had such a deep influence on her life.

"She was a strong woman, she had to be." said Barbara. "Besides raising me, she raised four sons, did all the cooking, gardening, sewing, and took care of the eighteen room Victorian mansion on Road 40, which her father built for her…later she took care of her mother when she became ill. When the house was destroyed by fire in 1966, she still had to take care of the farm."

Argolda Adams Kiplinger was born May 23, 1883 in a log cabin on the Rush/Henry County line. She was one of four daughters of S.B. Adams, a farmer and hatchery owner.

When Goldie, as she came to be called, was thirteen, her father built for her, a beautiful mansion which sat on the north side of Road 40. It was just west of Lewisville and for years, the site was known as the Fortieth Mile, a designation indicating that it was 40 miles to Indianapolis. Adams also erected the cement seats and the forty mile marker which still exists today, in front of the former site of the mansion.

Goldie grew into a formidable-looking young woman. She stood straight and seemed taller than her five- foot- four inches. She was active and intelligent, with brown eyes and an abundance of dark brown hair. Her many varied interests and talents made her a local renaissance woman. She attended Spiceland Academy, a school well known for its excellent teachers and outstanding curriculum.

Soon after she left school, she married Dunreith telegrapher, Ben Kiplinger.

Her granddaughter especially remembers her ability to make beautiful things with her hands. "She could create beauty out of nothing. She was a wonderful seamstress. She upholstered furniture, made custom drapes and all types of home accessories." Barbara remembers she had her first sewing lesson from her grandmother at age three. "Many times we stayed up way into the night sewing together."

"Grandma was fun to be with." remembers Barbara. "She had a sense of humor and kept you laughing." Goldie organized the R.S.T. Club, (rest, sew, and talk) which still exists today.

No one remembers exactly when Goldie began to display her mediumistic abilities. Once, when family members visited Camp Chesterfield, one of the mediums told them that their family contained a very talented medium. "We all knew she had to mean Grandma Goldie." said her granddaughter.

Barbara was well aware of her grandmother's talents. She vividly remembers seeing all of them displayed. Goldie was not afraid of her amazing abilities. She told Barbara. "Don't ever be afraid of them, they will not harm you." She also remembers her grandmother saying, "We are looked after, there are angels among us, and we don't know in what form they come."

One of Goldie's extraordinary talents was levitating objects. Once, she raised a large dining room table while Barbara was sitting on it. Barbara took this feat for granted as did most of the family regarding Goldie's unusual gifts.

"I saw her "witch for wells" many times." relates her granddaughter. "She would take a stick, a willow one, if she could find it. She would grip the prongs so hard sometimes, that her hands almost bled, but the stick would move and point downward, indicating the presence of water." Goldie often knew, not only where the water was, but how deep it was.

Goldie could also remove warts. "People would come from everywhere to have them removed." Barbara related. Goldie would go out to the driveway, pick up some stones, circle them around the warts, and then throw the stones over her shoulder. "It was the silliest thing to watch," Barbara chuckled, "but the warts went away."

Goldie was often aware of situations no one else knew about. She was once warned of danger by her deceased husband, Ben. She distinctly heard his voice tell her, "Go find Barbara now!" Goldie found her little granddaughter sitting on the cement bench in front of the house. She grabbed Barbara and ran inside. Moments later, a tramp passed by. Goldie was always convinced the man meant to harm her granddaughter, and that her dead husband's warning saved the child.

Their Victorian mansion was the site of mysterious events. Objects often came up missing. Goldie's husband, Ben, once saw Goldie's deceased father standing in the yard one day. He wore a brown suit just like the one he was buried in. Other unusual things happened. "We had an old glass bookcase that often popped and cracked and rattled and almost walked, it was so noisy." said Barbara. "The clock would be completely run down, and it would begin to chime and chime, sometimes twenty or thirty times."

One day in 1966, the mansion burned. Three days earlier, it had been hit by lightning. The family surmised that a spark ignited the timbers and caused the fire. Even after the house was gone, one of Goldie's sons, Joe, who still kept a garden there, could hear the phantom slamming of the old kitchen door as he tilled.

After the house burned, Goldie moved to Knightstown. She remained active and cheerful until the end. She died suddenly of a heart attack in 1969 at the age of eighty-six.

Fifteen years after her death, her son Joe, now living in California, heard the phone ring, one day. When he picked it up, he heard Goldie's voice at the other end. "Hello Joe, this is Mom." Argolda Adams Kiplinger, psychic extraordinaire, was still displaying her unique talents.

Haunted House at Flatrock

Janet Whitfield,* a Henry County resident, remembers the experiences she had many years ago in an old house at Flatrock, in Liberty township. This area has long been rumored to have several haunted houses.

Janet and her family lived in the old house in the 1940's. It was north of State Road 40, on one of the east-west county roads. It had six rooms and a dirt basement. She remembered it sat on a hill and was surrounded by a cement wall. There was an old cemetery near by.

Many unusual incidents occurred there which frightened her and her sisters. Footsteps would begin in an upstairs bedroom and someone could be heard walking down the stairs. As the footsteps reached the bottom, the door at the bottom of the steps would bang open and shut. No one was there. Janet's brother once saw a woman at the bottom of the steps, rocking and singing to a baby.

However, the scariest events took place in an upstairs bedroom which she shared with her sisters. This was the room from which the phantom footsteps emanated.

One evening, after going to bed, the girls heard deep breathing. "Is that you breathing?" Janet asked her sisters. "No," they replied. "Then we all held our breath. The breathing got even deeper. We all jumped up and ran downstairs.", she recalled. One night, after she was settled into bed, she happened to reach upward. She felt a hairy arm. She asked someone to turn on the light. The room was empty.

The unusual incidents continued but Janet and her sisters did not tell anyone. "Everybody knew about it." she said. "It was accepted as something that just happened and you lived with it." She doesn't know the history of the house or if anything tragic had occurred there. She and her family eventually moved away.

Over the years, she thought about the house and remembered how frightened she had been when she lived there. In 1972, she went back to see if she could find the house. It had been moved to a back field and was being used to store corn. It was later torn down. Today, the only reminder of the haunted house is a peaceful green field.

The Philo Southwick house in Lewisville, the site of unusual occurences

Monkeys and Bears

The Philo Southwick house in Lewisville was built in 1857. It is within yards of the old railroad which carried the Lincoln funeral train as it passed through Lewisville early on the morning of April 30, 1865. An old newspaper clipping, apparently now lost, pictured the house in the background as the train passed through. The clipping was on display at the Houston House a few years ago.

The red brick mansion sits atop a steep hill. Narrow stone steps led up to it. Some may call the house "haunted." but not unpleasantly so, according to owner, Jody Carnes. She does concede that some unusual things have happened there.

She recalls that, as a little girl she often stayed with her grandmother, who then owned the house. Carnes remembers waking one morning to see phantom bear cubs rolling and playing on the floor of a downstairs bedroom. She did not see them appear or disappear. She accepted the incident as routine and the bears did not seem threatening.

The living room was a place she always saw things and experienced unusual happenings. Once, she awakened to see a woman wearing prairie garb… a bonnet, and a drab calico dress. The woman walked up to Jody and held up her hand, which contained a butcher knife. "I started screaming and she just faded away." said Carnes.

Another time, when she was in this room, she looked around to see thin, spindle-legged monkeys on the stairwell nearby.

The monkeys, unlike the bears, scared her. She said, "They looked like they might hurt you… they were spider monkeys with little fez hats on their heads and red vests. They had long tails like monkeys you see at the circus."

There was a picture in the living room which gave her an eerie feeling. It was a drawing of a deer standing at a stream. When she watched the picture long enough, she saw the deer begin to walk across the stream. She didn't know who painted the picture or where it came from. It made her feel so uncomfortable, she gave it to a relative.

Strange things have happened in other areas of the house. Items were moved about. Once, her grandmother's sewing box had been placed in the middle of her bedroom doorway. The sewing box had been downstairs when she went to bed. Another time, a table belonging to her mother had been moved.

What lies behind the unusual happenings at the mansion? The appearance of the phantom bears and monkeys, she believes, may be due to a circus tragedy in some past era.... and the Southwick family suffered tragedies due to illness. Carnes says most of the Southwick children all died young of tuberculosis. "It was tragic, he (Philo Southwick) watched everyone he loved, die." she said. Many years ago, there was also a personal tragedy on the grounds, but she prefers not to talk about this.

Could these sad events have caused the unusual manifestations? Does the fact that the house (which contains hidden passageways and nooks) may have been used as an underground railroad, add to the likelihood of the paranormal incidents?

When asked if the phenomena are continuing, she replied, "Well, I thought things had quieted down." However, recently her five-year- old daughter refused to go up the stairs by herself. "She had never done that before." Carnes related. When she asked her little girl why she didn't want to go up the stairs, the child replied, "There are bad monkeys on the stairs."

"My heart just stopped." said Carnes. "I had not thought of those monkeys in years." She had never told her little girl about them. Yet, Carnes says the house is not frightening, and she is not unnerved by the incidents that have occurred there. She loves the house and intends to live there the rest of her life.

The potter's field grave of the murdered Miss F-32 at South Mound. Shown is a photo of the site taken by the author in January, 2004. Note the lightened misty area.

This highlighted photo shows the "face" in the mist. Could this "Lady in the Mist" be the murdered woman? The arrow in the picture points to a point of reference, the "ear-ring Orb". Credit: author's photo.   Highlighting: David W. Martin

Miss F-32

On a crisp fall day in 1932, Jesse Conrad and his son Eli, rumbled along in their truck on a side road near Lewisville, Indiana. Eli spied a large canvas object under a shrub on the roadside. When he went to inspect it, he noted a terrible stench. The Conrads immediately notified Lewisville town marshal, Fred Dishman, who after ascertaining that the bundle was a human body, called Henry County authorities. When Sheriff Ed Kirby and Prosecutor Eugene Yergin arrived, the canvas was transferred to the Macer Funeral Home.

There, Coroner Ralph Niblock discovered that the body was a young female between the ages of 20 and 30 years old. She was five-foot- four to five-foot- six inches in height, with dark brown or black hair. She was nude. Her left hand lay across her body and her long tapering fingers and well- manicured nails indicated she was a woman of some refinement. The canvas had been neatly wrapped around the victim's body and securely tied at the shoulders, waist and legs. Death was due to a crushed skull. Authorities surmised the woman died some months earlier, because of the advanced decomposition of the body. Eli Conrad recalled that he noted the foul odor along the roadside for some time, but had not been able to locate the source.

The next day, the woman was buried in potter's field in South Mound Cemetery. Her identity was given only as "Unknown". The grave site was labeled with a small stone tab labeled F-32. (Free ground, #32)

In the following days, the authorities worked to identify the woman. They checked with the Indianapolis and Cincinnati police. X-Ray photographs were made of the teeth in hopes of identifying the victim through dental work. The canvas was examined for clues. Prosecutor Yergin checked missing person lists and communicated with relatives who had missing girls. People came from nearby counties and even other states hoping to identify her.

No one seemed to know who she was. Authorities theorized that the woman had been killed in another area and her body dumped here. After three weeks, the story faded from the newspapers.

Police learned that in June, a complete woman's outfit had been found near Hagerstown. The clothing consisted of a red knit hat, white shoes, a black dress, lingerie and stockings. No one remembers if the clothing had identifying markers or tags. Those who found the clothing had thought it was inconsequential and disposed of it.

It was rumored that in the summer of 1932, an out-of-state car, resembling a gangster's car, was seen circling the area near where the body was found. Some say the victim later appeared as an apparition, and made a ghostly plea for help.

Yet, the woman was never identified and no one ever came to claim her remains. The case is still unsolved today, seventy-two years after her murder.

"….And Then There Were Eight."

Batson Cemetery, in Liberty Township, is one of the most beautiful and peaceful cemeteries in Henry County. Within its trimmed green lawns and stately old trees, sits a small white chapel. The cemetery, established in the 1830's, is the resting place of several prominent Henry County citizens, including Revolutionary and Civil War soldiers.

Co-existing with the cemetery's beauty are many tragic stories. Leota Penwell, a young New Castle woman, fell ill in 1913 shortly before her wedding. She died after an operation at a local hospital, and is buried there in her wedding dress. Nearby lies the grave of Kitty Heller, the first wife of an early New Castle florist, who died suddenly in 1905 after a short illness, at the age of twenty-nine.

A few years ago, a local couple redecorated the chapel in memory of their young daughter, who had been killed in an automobile accident shortly after visiting the cemetery. The girl had often come to the chapel in the cemetery to seek spiritual solace.

The cemetery was once known as "Hangman's Cemetery" because of certain overhead tree branches that caused the image of a hanging man to appear when automobile headlights were shined on nearby headstones. In the 50's, it was a favorite spot for teen boys to take their girl friends to scare them with the "hanging man apparition."

Like most cemeteries, it has a few ghost stories. One particular story began on Halloween night, 1997. Robert Binford and his family pulled up at the cemetery just after dark for an evening of scary fun. There were seven people in all. Binford, his wife Tonya, their three children, Binford's sister and her friend, Terry.*

The group climbed down from Binford's truck and walked about the lawns. Binford was telling the group that, "to kill a vampire, you use a chain saw." Unknown to his children, Binford and his father-in-law, Bob Swim, had arranged for Swim to secretly enter the cemetery with a chain saw, on which the chain had been dismantled.

"Just when I was telling them how you cut off vampires heads with a chainsaw, Bob turned on the saw." Binford related. "You never heard such yelling and screaming in your life" Binford chuckled. Tonya, Binford's wife, smiled and said, "Just at the time the chain saw started, a big flock of birds flew out of some pine trees nearby, making it even scarier. Our youngest son kept trying to turn on the flashlight. He kept wiggling it, but it kept going out."

"That was the fun part of the night." Binford continued. By that time, Binford's father-in-law had gone home and the group was left alone. They walked around in the middle part of the cemetery, which is surrounded by a circle drive.

Terry, the friend of Binford's sister, suddenly veered off from the group and fell behind. Binford saw her do this. "I knew she intended to hide behind a tombstone and jump out and scare us." he said. He called to her to let her know he had seen her. Binford noted that, when she got up to move, someone was behind her, in back of another headstone. When she got up to move, the figure moved with her. Binford, alarmed, yelled at the group to get to the truck because they were leaving

"I knew very well that who ever it was, it wasn't part of our group. I had counted all of us and I knew that with the other person, we had one too many. We scrambled to the truck and hightailed it home." he said.

That was more than six years ago and they haven't been back to the cemetery since. It's said that there have been incidents of vandalism at the cemetery. Perhaps such people should be warned that if they go to Batson Cemetery on a dark night, they may risk finding out who or "what" that eighth "person" is.

Murder Tract

The lights of the Beechwood Pavilion blazed brightly. Dancers swirled across the floor of the large ballroom. It was Friday evening, July 3, 1914. The Elks Club of Richmond, Indiana was celebrating Independence Day at the pavilion, located in Jackson Park on Road 40, west of Centerville, Indiana.

Among the one hundred guests was, Imogene Smith, a young New Castle woman.

She came to Richmond, with a group of other young people, as the guest of Ada and Grace Kelly of Richmond. All were planning to go to Cedar Point on Saturday to spend the holiday weekend.

After the orchestra played the last waltz, Imogene's group of six young people, climbed into a five passenger touring car driven by George Bayer of Richmond. Bayer quickly turned left onto Road 40. He intended to hurry to Richmond so they could reach a downtown restaurant before the other partiers.

His car was third in a long line of traffic coming from the pavilion. Bayer sped past the car in front of him and began to pass the lead car. As he did, the rear end of the car began to swerve. Witnesses later said it looked as if the wheel became entangled in an interurban track. Bayer turned the wheel sharply to the right, turned off the motor, and applied the emergency brake. This caused the car to overturn. Imogene Smith and Ada Kelly were hurled out, head first, both receiving fatal injuries.

The car landed in an upright position, its headlights still on, and glowing eerily through the darkness. The location was where Road 40 and Salisbury Road is today. The car was facing a plot of ground on the north side of the road ominously called Murder Tract, which had a one hundred year history of murder, suicide, and tragic accidents.

In the center of the tract of land sat a "haunted house", which had long been empty. Neighbors complained they often heard terrifying noises and screams coming from within the house. Cabinet doors flew open and banged against the walls. Attic doors never stayed shut.

A hanging, in1807, began the murder tract's gruesome history. Although the hanging occurred southeast of the tract, the gallows faced the house. In 1839, a neighbor girl was found murdered within the tract. The owner's son was acquitted, although his shoe fit the muddy footprint found near the dead girl, and blood had been found on his clothes.

In 1867, a man stabbed himself to death immediately after crossing the tract. He had encountered a farmer butchering hogs, picked up one of his knives, tested its blade, and then plunged it into his chest. In 1871, an owner's son was killed when hit by a falling tree limb. In this instance, the father had a premonition his son would die. For three nights prior to his son's death, he dreamed that a hearse, drawn by two black horses, pulled up to the house.

Tragic events continued to occur through the years. In 1872, there was a suicide by hanging, in 1889, an accidental death by gunshot. A short while before the automobile accident in which the young girls were killed, two Richmond men had been murdered by a neighbor, just south of the tract, in a feud over a boundary line.

Was it coincidental that the death automobile came to rest at the corner of the tract? Was the history of the tract's murders, suicides, and accidents connected to the tragic circumstances in which two talented and beautiful young girls lost their lives? Apparently, those who knew the history of the ill-fated ground, thought so. A few days after the wreck, articles about the history of Murder Tract appeared in both the Richmond Item and the New Castle Courier.

Friends, family, and victims may have had premonitions of the fatal car wreck as did some of the victims of Murder Tract.

It was learned that Ada Kelly, one of the dead girls, did not want to go the dance that evening, but acquiesced to please her friends. Michael Kelly, Ada's father, had declined to go to the dance. Lena Stretch, a New Castle girl, and a friend of Imogene Smith, also declined when Imogene asked her that Friday morning to accompany her to Richmond. The next time Lena saw her friend, it was to attend her funeral. It was by chance that George Bayer was driving the big touring car that evening. He offered his services, as a driver only a short time before the accident... and one wonders what became of the car, especially after learning that the Bayer family decided it was salvageable and intended to have it repaired.

Beechwood Pavilion , the dance hall from which the young people departed that night, still stands at 8502 National Road, and is now a private residence. The Historic Landmarks Foundation lists the pavilion, with its pyramidal roof and octagonal concession stand, as an outstanding example of entertainment and recreational architecture.

It is believed that part of the old Murder Tract still lies north and east of the present K-Mart store, and is bordered by the west side of Salisbury Road. Somewhere within that area was the former site of the haunted house. The old house has been gone for years and not many are likely to know of the sinister history of this land. It is hoped that its ominous reputation and its association with tragedy has long ago ceased.

WOODWARD BRIDGE   NEAR DUBLIN IND

Cry Woman's Bridge, originally called Woodward bridge, near Dublin, Indiana. It is said the cries of a woman are often heard as she looks for her baby. Now demolished. The road to the bridge is closed.   Credit: Dublin Sesquicentennial Book. 1830-1980.

Cry Woman Bridge

At the intersection of Golay and Heacock road, just south of Dublin, Indiana, is a weed-overgrown road, closed off now by an iron gate. It is the entrance to the much talked about Cry Woman Bridge. The bridge, which once stood about one-quarter mile down this road, was a large iron structure built about 1900. Only its pillars now mark the spot.

The legend of Cry Woman Bridge concerns the death of a young woman and her baby. Late on a rainy night, the woman was driving across the bridge with her infant child. She lost control of her car and mother and child plunged into the river below. The woman's body was found, but the only trace of the baby was a little blanket. No one knew where the woman was from, so she was buried in a pauper's grave along with the little blanket. Now, on foggy nights, the ghost of the woman is reportedly seen. Her cries and sobs are heard as she calls for her baby.

Is there any truth to the legend? Have local residents seen or heard the woman? A man who lives close to the bridge says the legend has a basis in fact. According to him, a woman and baby were killed here. "It was in the 50's or 60's. She is buried in one of the older cemeteries around here."

A Dublin man, James Reece, 35, remembers when he was a teen, he went to the bridge one night, with three other friends. They saw a white misty form emanate from the bridge area. "I couldn't tell if it was human, or a man or woman. We didn't hear anything." But he says the incident scared him and he hasn't forgotten it. "I used to hunt there before dawn, and I would hear noises coming from the bridge area, but I couldn't say if they had anything to do with the story."

A man living near the bridge says he believes some of the screams are caused by the wind going through culverts under the road leading to the bridge.

It may be hard to convince another Dublin resident of that. According to his wife, he apparently had a sinister experience at the bridge. When asked if she knew anyone who could verify hearing a woman scream or cry at the bridge, she replied, "My husband can, but he won't talk about it. He went out there one night and it scared him to death. At first he thought what he heard was the wind."

One of the older residents said he had been over the bridge a number of times. "But we always kept the windows closed." he related half-jokingly. An older woman resident related that she didn't "really much believe in the stories about the bridge." She did recall she had seen a number of young people go down to the bridge in a "macho" mood and come back looking very sober.

It seems that the legend is still alive and being given considerable respect. Not many living in the area would go down there on a dark night...if at all.

The staircase at the Sunflower Hotel, Camp Chesterfield, where the housekeeper encountered Miss Emma.   Credit :Photo printed with permission of the Board of Trustees of Camp Chesterfield.

"Miss Emma."

Camp Chesterfield, on the north side of the town of Chesterfield in Madison County, is rich in spirit-lore. The spiritualist center, in existence since the mid 1880's, draws hundreds of people from all over the country each year. They come to get readings and to take classes that develop their psychic abilities.

Quaint, turn-of-the-century cottages, dot the camp's thirty-four acres, along with beautiful religious statues, shady glens, and little stone bridges. A fountain sits in the center of the park. Jet black squirrels, said to be imported from France, scamper in the trees and on the lawns.

The center devotes itself to the training of spiritualist ministers and healers, and to the development of medium-ship. All visitors are welcome and seminars are conducted throughout the year. In 2000, the camp was placed on the National Historic Register.

Just inside the gates of the camp, sits the seventy-room Sunflower Hotel, built in 1914. It is the residence of one of Camp Chesterfield's most prominent spirits, "Miss Emma." Her real name is not known, but according to others, she's been around for years. A long- time visitor to the camp told of taking a photo many years ago of the hotel's housekeeper standing at the south end of the hotel porch. When it was developed, standing just behind the housekeeper, was a female figure in an old- fashioned dress. She seemed to be reading a letter. Could it have been Miss Emma?

Mary Beth Hattaway, head housekeeper at the camp, has seen Miss Emma. "I first saw her in 1994. She was descending the double staircase in the foyer of the hotel. She was coming down on my left as I was going up the staircase on the right. " says Hattaway. "She came about half way down the steps, then turned around and started back up and faded away." Miss Emma seemed to be quite at home and Hattaway believed that she was trying to impress upon her that the white glider-rocker in the upstairs lobby belonged to her. It's said that those who are familiar with the hotel, give wide leave-way to the white rocker. They say Miss Emma has been known to get upset if someone sits there without her permission.

Hattaway recalled Miss Emma's beauty. "She had skin like a porcelain doll's and her chestnut hair was done in an upsweep or bun. She was wearing an old- fashioned dress and appeared to be about forty years old."

Hattaway says there are other spirits at the Sunflower. One day she saw the "Colonel" out of the corner of her eye. "He was about 6:4. He wore a military outfit loaded with medals. Then, there is the "Doctor", who we think lives on the second floor. He only talks to very young children. We don't see him, but we hear the children answering his questions."

Yet, Hattaway believes Miss Emma remains the most elegant and intriguing spirit at the hotel. Who is Miss Emma? The housekeeper thinks she may be a former medium or visitor, who after passing away, just decided to stay on at the hotel because she loves it there. For those interested, it is said that Miss Emma is sometimes seen looking out an upstairs window on the second floor of the north side of the hotel.

Lova's doll house in Arlington Cemetery. Rush County.

The Legend of Lova's Doll-House

Lova Cline, a tiny invalid, lived at Arlington, Indiana in Rush County. Born in 1902, she had no muscular or neurological control of her body. She had never been able to sit up, could not bathe or fed herself and had to be carried everywhere. Her parents, George and Mary Cline, had tended to her every need since the day of her birth. Her only pleasure was gazing at the doll house built for her by her father.

The doll house, standing five foot high and weighing four hundred pounds, was filled with antique furniture made by her father. Lova's mother placed antique dolls in the house.

When Lova died in 1908 at the age of six, her father had the doll house moved to her grave site in the cemetery, nearby. The years passed, and a legend grew up around the little invalid girl and her doll house.

In 1945, Lova's mother passed away. George Cline wanted the doll house destroyed after her death, but the cemetery caretaker, Blount Sharp, persuaded him to let it remain in the cemetery. George Cline died in 1946. Lova's remains and the doll house were moved to her parents' gravesite.

Today, the white doll house with the gabled roof, sits under an old elm tree. Just beyond , is a small monument marking the site where Lova and her parents are buried. In front of the doll house is a plaque telling Lova's story, and a photograph of her in her casket, apparently the only known likeness of the little girl. A little purse and a toy beetle, tokens of affection from visiting children, are entwined in the metal stakes that support the plaque. People come from everywhere to see the doll house.

After the death of Lova's parents, the people of Arlington took care of the little house.

George Cline's will named his daughter's namesake, Lova Ward Wooten, as caretaker of the doll house.

Over the years, the house has been repaired and refurbished several times. Some years ago, it was taken to Tweedy's Lumber Company at Carthage and completely remodeled. The roof was replaced with metal, the cracks re-caulked, and the house was placed on a large foundation. Mrs. Wooten died in June, 1999 and the duty of caretaker passed to her daughter, Sheila Hewitt, of Arlington.

The doll house has been vandalized several times following newspaper stories about the legend. "Finally, we replaced the furniture and other articles with cardboard replicas and inexpensive furnishings." related Mrs. Hewitt. Since then, there has been no further vandalism. Mrs. Hewitt hopes that her granddaughter will take over the job of caretaker when she is gone.

Has anyone seen ghosts at the doll house? No...but a recent photograph of the doll house shows an "orb" (a shining ball of light that is thought to indicate a departed spirit.) hovering near the foundation. And, there is a legend that the house sometimes seems to be lighted from within at dusk, and that occasionally the little dolls in the house seem to be moved about, although the base of the house was bolted down over twenty years ago.

When asked about this, Mrs. Hewitt said she had never been aware of any paranormal activity. She smiled, as she said, "I'm the only one that takes care of the house and if I ever do see anything, they will have to find another caretaker."

Monument at the Simmons Cemetery, Hancock County, of Virginia and Alice Simmons, mysteriously poisoned at a family picnic in 1931.

Who Poisoned Virginia and Alice Jean?

The John Simmons family rolled along in their big sedan, going to a family picnic at Memorial Park in Lebanon, Indiana. It was Sunday morning, June 21, 1931. In the car with John, a prominent Hancock County farmer, was his wife, Carrie, their three daughters, Virginia 14, Alice Jean,10, Elizabeth, 16 and a family friend.

Wedged into an empty space on the floorboard of the back seat of the automobile, was a marshmallow tin containing twenty-one pressed chicken sandwiches. By 6 p.m. that evening, the happy group's lives would be changed forever. Two of the girls, Virginia and Alice Jean, would be dead from ingesting strychnine capsules that someone had placed in the sandwiches.

The party of six, after stopping for a short visit with relatives in Lebanon, arrived at the park about noon. The sandwiches were laid on a picnic table, along with food that other family members brought.

Virginia and Alice Jean were among the first to eat the sandwiches and become ill. Several other picnickers reportedly became ill, including John Simmons and Horace Jackson, Simmons' brother-in- law. Witnesses later commented that Carrie Simmons seemed strangely unconcerned about her daughters' symptoms. The girls were taken to nearby Witham Hospital where they both died later that evening.

Suspicion immediately centered on Mrs. Simmons. According to newspaper accounts, authorities apparently also thought Mr. Simmons knew more about the poisoning than he would tell and the press commented on his evasiveness and defensiveness with reporters. Mrs. Simmons was arrested and charged with murder the day after the funeral. She would be tried for the murder of her youngest daughter Alice Jean.

Since Lebanon was the county seat of Boone County, the trial took place there. It was a long affair lasting from September to

November. The family protested that their mother could not endure the time in jail and the stress of a trial. A doctor was consulted and concluded that the case could proceed.

Mrs. Simmons was lodged in the hospital section of the Lebanon jail. The Boone county sheriff and his wife tried to make her confinement more comfortable by giving her their best rocking chair. She was provided with a radio, on which she often listened to hymns. When her husband visited, they sang hymns together.

The neighbors were stunned at the charge against Mrs. Simmons. The family seemingly had a happy home life. They were an old, established farming family of Hancock County, and were good church members. John's neighbors supported him, even helping him plow his land so he could visit his wife in jail.

Carrie Simmons' family, including her oldest daughter, Elizabeth, and her two adult sons, George and Dale, staunchly supported her throughout the trial. It was thought that Mrs. Simmons' case might be hurt by the fact that her father was an inmate in a California mental institution for the killing of his second wife and step-son. The prosecutor would later question Carrie Simmons' mental stability.

The trial began in September and lasted five weeks. The prosecution's main thrust was that Carrie had bought strychnine three days before the poisonings. Charles Friedman, an Indianapolis druggist, was called to the stand and testified that on June 18, Mrs. Simmons was in his store and bought the poison. Mrs. Simmons conceded that she was in Indianapolis that day, but had gone there to shop with her husband and two younger daughters and to attend a charity function at Riley Hospital. The prosecution failed in their attempt to introduce into the record that Mrs. Simmons' grandfather had also apparently died mysteriously of strychnine poisoning.

Mrs. Simmons testified that she made the sandwiches the morning of the picnic and had placed a toothpick in each one. She contended that when she got to the picnic, she noticed that the toothpicks had been removed. But several at the picnic said they found sandwiches which contained two or three toothpicks.

The defense implied that someone, namely Simmons' brother-in-law, Horace Jackson, could have placed the poison in the sandwiches while the family was visiting relatives in Lebanon, before going on to the park. They maintained that Jackson's motive was revenge because the Simmons' testimony had been responsible for sending him to prison some years ago.

Jackson protested vehemently. Questioning of Jackson could not shake his story. It could not be proven that he had access to strychnine or to the sandwiches. Next door neighbors testified that they had been on their porch the whole time the Simmons family visited relatives at Lebanon, prior to going to the park, and that no one approached the automobile or the sandwiches.

To further complicate the case, the defense brought forth a female witness, who testified it was she, and not Mrs. Simmons, who bought the strychnine from druggist Friedman on June 18th.

John Simmons took the stand and told that he watched his wife make the sandwiches that Sunday morning in the kitchen, as he shaved. However, a barber in a nearby town, said that he had shaved Simmons on Saturday afternoon.

Mrs. Simmons was on the stand a day and a half. She denied that she had poisoned either child although she conceded that she made the sandwiches. She denied buying strychnine at Indianapolis. She cried, as she told how her daughter, Alice Jean, clung to her hand as she lay dying.

The case went to the jury in early November. They deliberated forty eight hours, but could not come to a unanimous decision. It was declared a "hung jury" and Mrs. Simmons was released on bond and eventually freed. Boone County authorities decided not to try her for the murder of her second daughter, Virginia, because of the time and expense.

The Simmons' returned to their farm home in Hancock County where they lived the rest of their lives. John Simmons died in 1949. Carrie Simmons died in 1969. They are buried near the double stone of their daughters, Virginia and Alice Jean, in the nearby Simmons cemetery.

Pearlie Guelsby with his aunt and uncle, Charles and Minnie Cooper.
Credit: Photograph courtesy of Christy White and family.

The Boy No One Remembered

It was a cold December day in Muncie, Indiana. The year was 1922. Fifteen-year-old Pearlie Guelsby Hogg, was on his way to school. Although his aunt, Minnie Cooper, with whom he lived, saw him leave, no one apparently saw him enter Muncie Central High School, where he was a sophomore.

When he did not return home that evening, his relatives reported him missing. His aunt and uncle tried for a time to find him, but being of modest means, their money soon ran out. They thought perhaps he had joined the service, as he had seemed dejected and unhappy recently. The months and years passed and Pearlie's whereabouts remained unknown.

On July 9, 1931, Otis Armstrong, a plumber, entered a vent stack at Muncie Central High School to repair a drain pipe. He entered the stack from the basement, crawling through an iron door and stepping into a darkened three by five area. His foot hit something hard, which he surmised was a brick. He shined his flashlight onto the object. He was startled to see that it was a human skull. Nearby, lay a skeleton, to which a few bits of dried flesh and cloth still clung.

The remains were taken to the Moffitt-Piepho Funeral Home. Authorities determined that the skeleton was a male between fourteen and sixteen years old. The bones were laid out in a box. Hundreds of people filed by, trying to make an identification. After seeing a knife and a shoe that had been found with the skeleton, an aunt recognized the remains as Pearlie's. General skeletal measurements, and the dark color of the few bits of hair that was found, also matched that of the missing boy.

Some wondered why the decaying of the body had not caused an odor. Officials explained that there were ventilating fans at the top of the vent that circulated the air upward through the shaft and into the outside of the building.

How had Pearlie gotten into the shaft? Had he jumped? Had he fallen in accidentally? Had he been pushed?

Several conjectures were put forth. He could have been involved in horseplay and perhaps fallen in accidentally. His uncle Charley did not think so. "Pearlie was a serious boy. He was not given to horseplay." said the man. He suggested someone who had a grudge might have pushed him in. He heard that some of the boys had a feud with a teacher. Could Pearlie have been part of such a dispute? No evidence of this was ever offered. Could he have been smoking in the narrow passageway, as some of the boys did and accidentally fallen into the shaft? But, Pearlie did not smoke.

Stories from other sources began to point to a sadder possibility. Pearlie recently told a neighbor he planned to run away or to kill himself because he was severely treated at home. Those who knew the family said he was often whipped, and that his aunt was unusually strict with him. He told a Muncie police officer he was tired of life and that "one of these days, you will find me in the stone quarry."

Pearlie's life had been harsh since birth. He was born near Eldorado, Illinois in 1907. His father left the family before he was born. His mother died soon after his birth. At four, he went to live with his aunt and uncle in Muncie, Indiana. He possessed a solemn and industrious nature. He attended school during the day and drove a delivery wagon until nine at night. Roger Maher, his employer, who also made a positive identification of Pearlie at the funeral home, stated that Pearlie was "a fine boy, absolutely honest and a good worker."

After a two day investigation, Coroner Clarence G. Piepho came to his conclusion. On the death certificate, he listed the cause of death as, "probable suicide."

Although everyone apparently forgot about Pearlie during the years he was missing, the city of Muncie gave him a proper burial. Elm Ridge Cemetery donated a plot. He received a marker from the Busch, Russell and Geits Company. Graveside rites were performed by Rev. Arthur W. McDavitt, pastor of the St. John's Universalist Church.

The little cortege left the funeral home at 9:40 a.m. on July 11, 1931. It's said that Dick Green, later a reporter for the Muncie Star, and a contemporary of Pearlie's, was a pallbearer. He, reportedly, found it a saddening experience, saying, "no coffin should have been as light as Pearlie's."

The room in the Scott Opera House, Fairmount, Indiana, where most of the unusual phenomena occurred. On the far left is a small white "orb" in which some say they can see a man's face.

Phantoms of the Opera?

As most lovers of the paranormal know, an opera house is a favorite hangout for a ghost. The old Scott Opera House at Fairmount, Indiana, built in 1884, may be one such place. Levi Scott, a prominent Fairmount, Indiana businessman, was the original owner. The building still stands today and occupies the second floor of 116 South Main Street. It was once a state-of-the-art theatre, containing 2500 square feet, with sixteen foot ceilings, and a commodious stage.

In later years, it was used for musical performances, plays and readings. James Whitcomb Riley appeared there in 1893. More recently, it was used for the manufacturing of small auto parts, and later for storage. It is on the National Register of Historic Places and plans are being made to renovate it for community meetings and activities.

If a group of local youths hadn't needed a place for their band rehearsals a couple of years ago, no one would be aware of the unusual happenings there. After the teens began rehearsals, strange events took place.

Apparently, one of the youths relayed the eerie experiences to his mother, Judy Cowling, president of Historic Fairmount. According to Mrs. Cowling, the teens told her they witnessed skate boards and other objects being moved. A large family Bible flew off a table and across the room. A coiled wire, which lay on top of an amplifier, began to move upward in the air, as if reacting to a snake charmer.

One teen girl saw the apparition of a man standing in one of the doorways. Apparitions appeared at the other upstairs entrance, and at the top of the stair well which leads from the street to the second floor. An invisible force apparently kicked an empty guitar case hard enough to break the strap. All the phenomena occurred after dark and usually happened only once.

Cowling remains skeptical. "I don't believe I have observed enough phenomena to make a judgment on whether the building is haunted." she related in an interview on November 26, 2003.

Some have photographed "orbs" in the building, (white ovals of light that some paranormal researchers believe are evidence of departed spirits) and in some of the photographs, there appear to be unusual formations. Cowling thinks the orbs could be dust, and she believes the unusual formations may be wallpaper patterns, or that they have a reasonable explanation.

One night, Cowling went to the opera house to see for herself. It was near midnight, and the teens were there, as well as several adults. She stayed about two hours. She concedes that she got locked behind a door that had been previously unlocked, and acknowledges that she could not get out until someone helped her open the door. She still remains non-committal about the experience, saying that she could have been tired or inattentive that evening.

There have been several newspaper stories about the happenings at the opera house. The South Bend Ghost Trackers were there in the spring of 2003, but apparently found nothing.

The band has long since departed from the building and is rehearsing elsewhere. They did not find the experiences threatening or evil. They think its "cool", and don't know what the fuss is all about.

Will the "phantoms" (if that is what they are) make their appearance again? We will probably have to wait until the renovation of the opera house is complete, to find out.

The Israel Jenkins House near Fairmount, Indiana. Built in 1845. Now used as a clubhouse for golfers. Some say they have had eerie experiences there.

Ghosts on the Green

Sara and Randy Ballinger are the owners of the Walnut Creek/Club Run Golf Course, located a few miles northeast of Fairmount, Indiana. For several years, they have had reports of eerie happenings at the Israel Jenkins house, which lies within the area of the golf course. The Greek Revival house, built in 1840, is on the National Register of Historic Places. It now serves as a clubhouse for the golfers at Walnut Creek.

The paranormal incidents began in the late 1980's when the Ballingers purchased the Jenkins house and their daughter heard unusual noises there. It was during its restoration a few years ago, that the unusual phenomena escalated.

A workman, who had been working nights at the house, reported feeling that someone was watching him. One evening, as he was busy at a task, the hair on his arms suddenly stood up. He then heard a little boy's voice distinctly tell him, "Get out of here!" After this incident, he refused to work in the house at night. The Ballingers believe the workman was not a man easily frightened. "He was a marine and a Viet Nam vet." related Sara Ballinger.

Others report they hear footsteps going up and down the stairs, see doorknobs turning and hear doors closing, yet there is never anyone there. Not long ago, a group of lady golfers outside the house saw someone watching them from an attic window. But, the Ballingers say no one goes into the attic, and the door that leads to it is always padlocked. The house was recently checked by the Ghost Trackers, but apparently nothing unusual was found. Randy Ballinger says the Society thought there were too many curious onlookers that day for unusual phenomena to manifest.

What could be causing the paranormal events? Randy believes the house might have been a center for the Underground Railroad. There are also Indian mounds, and nearby burial grounds. Indian artifacts have been found in the creek... all circumstances which sometimes encourage manifestations of the paranormal.

Have any tragedies occurred in the house or on the grounds? A nine-year-old boy, Lewis, a member of the Jenkins family, is thought to have died in the house or on the grounds many years ago. Randy thinks he may have possibly drowned in the nearby creek. A Jenkins son was killed in the Civil War, and is buried in the Savannah, Georgia National Cemetery. Could these incidents contribute to the unusual happenings within the house?

Whatever the cause, the Ballingers seem content to let things remain just as they are. Apparently the "ghosts" or whatever they are, do not upset the daily routine of the Ballingers or the golfers who use the house for their meetings and luncheons.

The James Dean portrait done by a New York man, many years ago. It is said that the portrait fell from a closet and broke at the moment of Dean's death. Credit: Photograph courtesy of David Loehr of the James Dean Gallery. Gas City, Indiana.

James Dean's Portrait

In 1990, David Loehr, owner of the James Dean Gallery at Gas City, Indiana, received a unique gift. It was a five-by-seven pastel portrait of James Dean, drawn by Tony Lucev, a New York man. Lucev had sketched it as a teenager. A letter accompanied the portrait, stating that there was an unusual story associated with it.

Lucev said he did not know of James Dean until after his death in an automobile accident in California. He later saw Dean's movie "East of Eden" and was so impressed with the actor's role as "Cal Trask" that he saw the movie several times.

At the time, he was studying to be an artist, and felt compelled to draw the portrait of Dean. He used a photograph of Dean as his guide. After completing the portrait, he placed it in a glass frame. Because he hadn't yet decided where to hang it, he placed the framed portrait in his upstairs closet, laying it in a flat position.

According to Lucev, on September 30, 1956, about 10 p.m., Eastern Daylight Savings Time, he and several members of his family were downstairs in the kitchen when they heard a loud crash from upstairs. When Lucev went upstairs to check, he found his closet door open. The portrait of Dean was on the floor with the glass broken.

Apparently suspecting that a paranormal event may have occurred, he checked a magazine for Dean's death hour, and found that the actor's death occurred at 5:59 p.m. He shrugged the incident off because the time difference between his time (10 p.m.) and California time (7 p.m.) was three hours, and not four hours as it should have been for the EDST time zone.

However, years later, when he mentioned the incident to a friend, the friend told him that California goes off daylight savings time the last Saturday in September. In 1956, this would have been September 29, 1956, meaning that on September 30, 1956, when the portrait broke, the four hour difference would have been in effect between

California and New York time. Thus, the portrait did, indeed, fall at the same moment of Dean's death. (within one minute)

Yet, Lucev apparently did not realize that Dean had died on September 30, 1955 and not September 30, 1956. The portrait fell at the exact moment of Dean's death, but one year later.

In 1958 Lucev sent his information to the Parapsychology Laboratory at Duke University. He received an answer from Dr. Louisa Rhine, a nationally-known scientist at the university, who with her husband Dr. J.B. Rhine, headed parapsychology studies at Duke.

After thanking him for his contribution, Dr. Rhine noted that she believed the incident was a very unusual coincidence. She then posed the question that he may have been mistaken about the year he drew the picture, since in most cases a falling object and a death occur at the same time, rather than a year apart.

Could Lucev have been mistaken about the year? The movie "East of Eden" was released in the March of 1955, so Lucev could have seen it in 1955 rather than 1956. However, it still remains an amazing coincidence that the picture broke at the exact moment of Dean's death.

Today, Lucev's portrait of Dean, along with his letter to Loehr, and his reply from Dr. Louisa Rhine, hang in the James Dean Gallery and is seen by thousands of people each year.

On the left: the "ghost" of the fifth street bridge.   Credit: Photograph by Kimball Hendrix. Reprinted with permission of the Connersville News-Examiner.

The Ghost of the Fifth Street Bridge

On an overcast morning in May, 1990, Kimball Hendrix, then a reporter for the Connersville News- Examiner, snapped a photograph of the East Fifth Street Bridge in Connersville.

When the photograph was developed, Hendrix realized he had taken a picture of a very unusual image. On the bridge, in the left of the photograph, was what appeared to be a blocky, monk-like figure, a cowl apparently covering its head. The form seemed to be striding diagonally across the bridge, and about to walk into the swollen Whitewater River, several feet below.

Many people telephoned about the eerie image. Apparently, some callers questioned the validity of the photograph, perhaps thinking it could have been tampered with, or that rain, or an imperfection in the negative, could have produced the figure. All of these possibilities were checked and ruled out. There was no sun that day, ruling out the possibility of the play of sunlight. The lens was clear, the negative unmarred. No one had retouched the photograph.

Other callers were not surprised to see the image. It seems that according to several, the area around the bridge had long had a reputation of being haunted. One lady caller commented, "It's the ghost. There has always been a ghost over there, and now there is a picture to prove it."

Who is the "ghost" and what is his purpose? No one seems to know. The old bridge has been around for many a year, so there could be many tragic or poignant personal stories connected to it. It is rumored that there was at least one suicide at the bridge, many years ago.

The original bridge was built at that site in the late 1830's, and then replaced by a long covered bridge, built by Archibald Kennedy in 1884. In this era there was a boating and picnic area on the east bank. Nearby was an old ball park. Was the "ghost" being drawn back these nostalgic times?

The covered bridge was razed in 1934 and the present concrete bridge was built the next year. Today, the remnants of the bridge's colorful past are gone. It is just a busy thoroughfare which spans the Whitewater River. The thick growth of trees and shrubs, which surrounded it when the photograph was taken, has now been cleared away. If the "ghost" appears again, "he" will certainly be easy to see.

Kimball Hendrix, the photographer who took the picture, was contacted recently at his home and remembered the incident.

Hendrix recalled, "I was not on assignment when I took the picture. I went down there because I was told something was down there. People were seeing a vision or a biblical figure." He remembered that the photograph seemed to generate a discussion of "good and evil." "It was definitely a unique situation for me, an eerie situation. I felt that the "presence", whether good or evil, was real."

The Wilson Bridge, Randolph County. Built in 1883 by A.M. Kennedy. Now demolished. This bridge closely resembles the one in the hatchet lady legend. Credit: "Covered Bridges on the Byways of Indiana." Bryan E. Ketcham.

The Legend of the Mad Hatchet Lady

A well-known Randolph County legend is that of the Mad Hatchet Lady, who is said to have haunted the area around one of the county's old covered bridges, many years ago. The story goes that she lived in a tin hut at the end of a forked road. Apparently, she was an angry and demented woman, who roamed the woods at night, carrying a hatchet, and threatening anyone who came near.

On full moon nights, people were said to be safe because she stationed herself in the rafters of the nearby covered bridge and screamed at anyone who was unlucky enough to come through. Many times, teens would drive out from surrounding small towns to catch a glimpse of her or to hear her scream.

No one knows what happened to her or why she behaved as she did. Perhaps, she was senile or frightened, and trying to protect herself.

The exact site of the bridge is not known. Of the six covered bridges that Randolph County once had, one, the Wilson Bridge, comes closest to fitting the description of the bridge the Mad Hatchet Lady reportedly haunted. The bridge was built in 1883 by A.M. Kennedy, the famous Indiana bridge builder. It had a tin roof and the sides were wooden shingles. It was located near the town of Farmland, and nearby, was a forked road called Angle Road. Was this the forked road where the mad hatchet lady lived in her tin hut? According to a Farmland resident, the bridge burned many years ago and a narrow, slim-lined bridge has taken its place.

Now that the Hatchet Lady has no rafters to sit on, perhaps she is still roaming the woods nearby, hatchet in hand.

References

1. The Mysterious Disappearance of Catherine Winters. New Castle Times. New Castle Courier. New Castle Democrat. Richmond Palladium. Richmond Evening Item. Indianpolis News. Indianapolis Star. The Cincinnati Post. (March 21, 1913- December 31, 1914.)

2. Little Ghost Girl. Personal Interview, March 13, 2003. Library Research.

3. To Those Who Walked These Grounds. Personal Interviews, January 18, 2003, January 20, 2003, March 13, 2003, July 19, 2003, February 18, 2004. Henry County Interim Report, Historic Landmarks Foundation. 1993. pp 25-28. Edric Thay. "The Little People." Ghost Stories of Indiana. Ghost House Books. Canada. 2001. pp. 159-161. David Mannweiler. "Home Grown Ghosts." Indianapolis Star. October 27, 1996.

4. The Amorous Ghost. Personal Interview. June, 2003. Library Research.

5. The Repentant Friend. Personal Interview. March 3, 2003.

6. The Bundy Madstone. Personal Interview. September 13, 2003 with Edna Mae McKee and Kelly Ellington. "Edna McKee Tells Bundy Madstone Story." Fran Richardson, Courier Times. September 30, 1978. "Bundy Madstone Once Credited With Effecting Cures." Betty O'Neal Giboney, Courier Times, May 23, 1963. " Indiana Scientists Assail Alleged Madstone." Indianapolis News. October 30, 1909.

7. The Black Cloud. Personal Interview. January 7, 2003.

8. Our Little Friend. Personal Interview. February 22, 2003.

9. The House That Spoke. Personal Experiences of the Author. 1988-1995.

10. The Haunted Apartment. Personal Interview. January 23, 2003; May 29, 2003.

11. The Spectre Nurse and the Man in Black. Personal Interviews. January 20, 2003. July15, 2003. Personal interviews on March 12, 2004 with Keith Burkman R.N. and Dianne Mercer-Elmore R.N.

12. The Tavern Ghost. Personal Interview. August 22, 2003. Library Research.

13. Monkey Jack Bridge. Personal Interview, July 6, 2003, March 26, 2003, Telephone Interviews. August 29, 2003. August 30, 2003. "Henry County Rich with Folklore." Lisa Pfenninger, Courier Times, October 24, 1984.

14. Mt. Lawn Mansion. Biographical Memoirs of Henry County, Indiana. B.F. Bowen, 1902. Personal Interviews with Judy Bowling-Hyatt, February 11, 2003, April 5, 2003. June 28, 2003. "Occult Activities Seen on Rise in Henry County." Eldon Pitts, Muncie Star. October 30, 1988. "House at Mount Lawn Had Strange Goings On In The Old Days." Courier Times. July 26, 1951. Satanism, "The Devil Made Me Do It." Is A Phrase Now Under Study. Henry County News Republican, May 4, 1989.

15. Molly and Her Baby. New Castle Democrat. July-November, 1904. November, 1905. Rushville Repubican, November,December, 1904. December, 1905. Indianapolis Star, September, 1952.

16. Which Way to Mooreland? Personal Interview. November 21, 2003.

17. Death Car. Personal Interview. March 23, 2003.

18. John Payne's Spirit Portrait. New Castle Democrat, August 25, 1905. New Castle Courier, August 24, 1905. Irene Swan, "The Bangs Sisters and Their Precipitated Portraits." 1969. Reprint. 1991.

19. Lady In Black. (Pest House) "Adventures in Buying the Pest House." Rhoda Hamblin, Courier Times, July, August. 1999. Interment Records, Glen Cove Cemetery, Knightstown. Interment Records. New Castle Health Department. Personal Interview. February, 2003. "Couple Matter of Fact About What Happens in Old House." Eldon Pitts, Muncie Star Press. October 5, 1997.

20. Who Was Skara Brae? "Death of Local Reclusive Woman a Mystery." Mark Tabb, Knightstown Banner. October 23, 2002. Personal Interview, November 19, 2003. Henry County Interim Report. Historic Landmarks Foundation. 1993. p. 153.

21. Dream of Death. New Castle Daily Times. December 17, 1912.

22. Goldie Kiplinger, Lewisville Medium. Personal Interview with Barbara Meade, October 24, 2003. "This Old House." Darrell Deck, National Road Traveler. January 22, 1998.

23. Haunted House At Flatrock. Personal Interview. August 19, 2003.

24. Monkeys and Bears. (Philo Southwick House) Personal Interview with Jody Carnes. August 25, 2003. Library Research.

25. Miss F-32 . New Castle Courier Times, October 6-14, 1932. Interment Record, South Mound Cemetery.

26. And Then There Were Eight. Personal Interview with the Robert Binford family. October 24, 2003. Library research.

27. Murder Tract. New Castle Courier. New Castle Times. Richmond Evening News. Richmond Palladium Item, July 4-8, 1914. Richmond Palladium Item. July 9, 1914. New Castle Courier, July 16, 1914. Wayne County Interim Report. Historic Landmarks Foundation of Indiana. 2001. p.125.

28. Cry Woman Bridge. Personal Interview. Dublin Sesquicentennial Book. 1830-1980. p. 123. Beth Scott and Michael Norman. "Haunted Heartland." Warner Books. 1985. pp. 86-87.Interviews with local citizens. June, 2004.

29. Miss Emma. Personal Interview with Mary Beth Hattaway, December 23, 2003. Camp Chesterfield Lives, Our First Hundred Years. 1886-1986

30. The Legend of Lova's Doll House. Personal Interview with Sheila Hewitt, February 14, 2004. Rushville Repubican, February11, 1980? No author. No title. " Memory of Little Girl Lives in Cemetery." C.J. Wilson, Shelbyville News. No date. "New Dollhouse Nestled on Cemetery Plot Perpetuates Memory of Doomed Child." Joe Adams, Indianapolis Star. October 30, 1949.

31. Who Poisoned Virginia and Alice Jean? Greenfield Republican, June-November, 1931. Lebanon Reporter. June/July 1931. Dorothy June Williams and Thomas Earl Williams. A History of Greenfield in the 20th Century. Coiny Press. No date. Pp.261-263.

32. The Boy No One Remembered. Muncie Star, July10, 1931. Muncie Press, July 9-10, 1931. "Our Neighborhood." Dick Green, Muncie Star. March 16, 1983. "Old CHS Mysteries Recalled." Dale Burgess, paper? (Files of the Muncie Genealogy Center.) February 28, 1973. Telephone interview with Christy White, relative of Pearlie Guelsby, February 12, 2004.

33. Phantoms of the Opera? Fairmount Public Library. Personal Interviews with Judy Cowling, November 16, 2003; November 26, 2003. "Local Opera House Has Its Own Phantom." Cathy Shouse. Chronicle Tribune. Marion. June 7, 2003. "Jittery Students Think Opera House Haunted." Muncie Star Press. June, 2003.

34. Ghosts on the Green. Personal Interview with Randy and Sara Ballinger, November 26, 2003

35. James Dean's Portrait. Personal Interview with David Loehr, November 18, 2003. Copies of letter of Tony Lucev to David Loehr. Dr. Louisa Rhine's reply to Tony Lucev. Dec.10,1958.

36. The Ghost of the Fifth Street Bridge. Photograph by Kimball Hendrix, Connersville News-Examiner. May 16, 1990. P.1c.1-4. Kimball Hendrix article. Connersville News-Examiner. May 24, 1990. P.10 c.2-3. Telephone interview with Kimball Hendrix, May, 2004.

37. Legend of The Mad Hachet Lady. "The Legend of Spooky Hollow and The Mad Hatchet Lady." William Jackson, October 28, 1978. newspaper not identified. (from the Anna Lou Arnett Collection, "A Glimpse of the Past.") Lynn Library. "Covered Bridges on the Byways of Indiana." Bryan E. Ketcham, "Covered Bridges on the Byways of Indiana." Oxford Printing Company. Oxford, Ohio. 1949. P.160. Back Cover: Photograph (2x3) of author. Credit: Photo: Barbara Cross.

About the Author

Charlene Z. Perry is a retired registered nurse and licensed massage therapist. She has long been interested in parapsychology, mysteries and ghostlore. She lives in a small apartment in Henry County with her cat, Lily.

Printed in the United States
65783LVS00010B/252

9 781418 485740